CW01560674

A jewel of a book, packed wi
to achieve that most elusiv
quiet. Offering guidance for t.
silence for themselves and
wanting to run Quiet Days in their local situation. For
those faced with a demanding world, 'Quiet' is a
practical guide to calm the cacophony of noise and
listen attentively to the still, small voice of God.
Bishop Adrian Newman, Chair of the
St Benedict's Centre

'Quiet' says everything about this book and the
passion of its author. Using her own story, Margaret
takes us on a journey of understanding into the
importance of creating space in our own lives for
quiet. She does this with biblical insights, practical
examples and humour. She provides helpful
materials to establish a personal rhythm of quiet in
the midst of busyness, whether alone or with others.
In the hyperactive world we inhabit, many will be
drawn by the very word "quiet" and will find here an
oasis of spiritual refreshment for their thirsty souls.
Tony Horsfall, Author of Attentive to God

I am delighted to recommend 'Quiet' to anyone
seeking wise and practical guidance in their search
for quiet space in which to nurture their relationship
with God. Margaret's wealth of personal experience
shines through. I hope it will encourage those
seeking the quiet that is so hard to find in modern
life.
Anne Clarke OSB, Abbess of Malling Abbey

In the busyness of modern life in the twenty-first century, taking time to be quiet is an act of resistance. May you rediscover the lost spiritual discipline of quietness as you engage with this timely book.
Mike Royal, General Secretary of Churches Together in England

QUIET

A Guide to Spending Time
with God in a Demanding World

Thanks

I am immensely grateful to all those who have encouraged me on my journey of faith, most notably the late Katie England. Particular thanks must go to those who have attended and encouraged me in the Quiet Days that I have led. Special thanks to Sal, Barbara and Miriam, my cheerleaders. Finally, to Mandy Carr, Tony Horsfall, Susanne Carlsson and Matt Bird for helping bring this book to print and not letting it remain a pipe dream.

Contents

Introduction

Chapter 1   Why Take Time to Be Quiet? The Importance and the Biblical Principles

Chapter 2   What Is a Quiet Day and What Does it Mean to Be Intimate with God?

Chapter 3   Who Might Benefit from a Quiet Day?

Chapter 4   How to Use a Quiet Day. How Might We Hear God's Voice and How Do We Avoid Distractions?

Chapter 5   Where and When to Find Quiet

Chapter 6   Planning a Quiet Day—A Practical Guide

Chapter 7   Introduction to Resources

Resource 1   Advent 1: Obedience

Resource 2   Advent 2: The Gifts of the Magi

Resource 3   Lent 1: Last Words

Resource 4   Lent 2: Temptations of Jesus

Resource 5   Holy Week: Four Men Who Bore Crosses

Resource 6   Jesus Appears to the Disciples

Resource 7   Zacchaeus

Resource 8   God's Workmanship

Resource 9   Harvest: Jesus Is the Vine

Author Biography

Foreword

We live in an age where so many people want things to move faster. Our "enjoy now, pay later" culture is consuming us. The evidence is all around us—a pandemic of mental illness, relational strains like never before and more instability in our social structures than ever before. At the same time, there is a ground swell for something better and something deeper—a desire to find a way of walking at a pace that is sustainable and healthy.

In 'Quiet', Margaret opens up the ancient wells of scripture and Christian spirituality. She reminds us, in the words of the late Kosuke Koyama, that we serve a "three-mile-an-hour" God. She invites us, lovingly and firmly, into a better place and a deeper purpose. Her words are crafted from the depths of her own experience and encounters with Christ. She not only writes of this better rhythm and deeper well, she lives it.

I invite you to read her words and to meditate on them, allowing the sap of hope to rise in your soul as you sink into the song of God's grace.

Rev Malcolm Duncan

Senior Minister at Kensington Temple London

MARGARET WOODING JONES

Introduction

As a small child in primary school, I vividly remember being captivated by stories from the Bible. Although I enjoyed all our story times, there was something about the Bible stories we were reading that sparked my imagination like no other book. However, it was not until I came to a living faith in Jesus in my mid-teens that the Bible truly came alive for me. I read it with a hunger and a passion, and as I did, I developed an incredible desire to share what I was reading and learning with others.

You might wonder what I mean by "a living faith in Jesus". Some people have a profound, life-changing encounter; others reach the end of themselves and cry out to God in pure desperation. But my experience was quite different and developed over a long period. Like many others of my generation, I assumed that because I was born in England and went to church as a child at Christmas and Easter, I was already a Christian. It was only when I joined the local church youth group that I realised something completely different. There, I met strangers—who were genuinely kind and caring, interested in my thoughts and feelings. They looked out for everyone, not just their close friends. There were no cliques or groups, nor the gossip and rumours that often marked my daily experience at an all-girls secondary school. They behaved very differently, and I wanted to understand what motivated this kindness. Through their care and, inevitably, their prayers for me, I experienced firsthand a living faith and some remarkable answers to those prayers. Here, I encountered a God who listened to and responded to the prayers of very ordinary individuals who believed and trusted in Him. One night, in the privacy of my bedroom, I committed my life to Jesus and resolved to follow wherever He might lead me. It has been a lifelong adventure that has taken me to places I could never have imagined, providing opportunities to utilise gifts and talents that might otherwise have remained hidden.

'Quiet' encompasses these two fundamental elements that started my Christian journey and remain central to my life: a passion for the Bible, the living Word of God, and a passion for prayer. A third element might be my strong desire to encourage others to experience the richness of these interactions themselves—not merely amidst the busyness of everyday life but by exploring the value of finding God in quiet places. Throughout my life, in both work and ministry, I have treasured moments to pause and reflect. It is often in those times of quiet stillness that God speaks most clearly.

'Quiet' is for everyone, regardless of age, gender or race. I believe that each of us is uniquely made and cherished by our Creator. Therefore, it follows that we would want to draw closer to Him and seek His words of wisdom for our lives, or, like two lifelong companions who are comfortable simply sitting together in silence, to just "be present" with Him. It is a sad reality that most Quiet Days are mainly, though not solely, attended by women. Where are the men?

Come and help to address this imbalance; come and discover the wonderful, life-giving, life-restoring benefits of retreating and being still for a while.

It is also true that Quiet Days tend to attract people of a certain age. Where are our young people? You have nothing to fear. Don't believe that time spent apart with God is only for those who have their lives sorted out. Firstly, we haven't! Secondly, this is all the more reason to pause and seek guidance and support along the way. We only need to look to the Bible to see that God loves to speak to young people and has sometimes trusted them with incredible visions to follow. King David was just a boy when he learned to trust God while shepherding the sheep. Gideon was a frightened young man when God appeared to him hiding in the winepress and Mary was likely only a teenager when the angel Gabriel announced she was chosen by God to bear the Messiah. And let's be honest, Jesus was only 30 when He began His ministry, and, as we shall see, He spent plenty of time alone with God.

Whoever you are—introvert or extrovert, young or old, happy or sad—'Quiet' is for you. Quiet Days are beneficial for everyone; they offer an opportunity for anyone to step aside for a while, to be still and to listen.

The book can be used individually with additional questions to consider or as a group study resource, with each chapter ending with discussion prompts. The reader will examine the issues faced and the benefits gained from discovering a rhythm of quiet space.

Many church communities are exploring and supporting the importance of organised Quiet Days, which can easily be arranged locally. 'Quiet' dedicates two full chapters to successfully organising a Quiet Day and provides ample resources for those unfamiliar with where to start.

My prayer is that if you have not yet experienced the benefits of quiet and stillness with God, you will feel inspired to try it for yourself. And if you have, may you feel empowered to encourage others to join you on that journey.

Note: I am aware that throughout the book, I have referred to God in the masculine. This is for the sake of simplicity, although I recognise that some may find this challenging. However, I am deeply conscious that God's very nature and character include everything maternal as well as paternal. A mother's love may serve as a more helpful image for some.

Chapter 1

Why Take Time to Be Quiet? The Importance and the Biblical Principles

"Be still and know that I am God"
(Psalm 46:10).

"Why take time to be quiet?" is a good question to start with; we all live in a world that is bombarded by noise, both from outside ourselves and within. It is virtually impossible to find a space where some form of noise does not invade our ears or minds. Even as I write this, my phone buzzes for my attention (skillfully ignored by switching to aeroplane mode), and immediately afterwards, someone is at my front door (less skillfully ignored!). Beyond these everyday familial distractions, the world hurls at us a myriad of noises over which we have no control, despite our brains' ability to filter them out temporarily. These include traffic noise, police sirens, barking dogs, slamming doors or a television. Even if you live alone in a rural idyll, I suspect you can still hear distant farm machinery or an aeroplane overhead as well as the birdsong and animals bleating or braying. Take a moment to listen and acknowledge all the different sounds around you—it may be as simple as hearing a clock ticking, the dishwasher emptying or the hum of a fan. In addition to all that background noise, there is the mental bombardment we readily succumb to, whether from hearing too much in the news or scrolling through social media; our minds are often cluttered with unhelpful and unnecessary thoughts. All of this occurs before we even consider personal stressors: family issues, work pressures, financial worries, health concerns, busy schedules and so on. How many of us have thought at times, "Stop the world, I want to get off!"? Or simply, "Just give me five minutes of peace!" Sadly, far too many seek that peace in the wrong way, a common one being, "Let me just sit with a glass of wine." While there's nothing wrong with a glass of wine, it won't fundamentally alter your circumstances. So, are we aiming for the impossible? What if you could find an inner peace amid everything happening around you—one that could support you through the noise, activity and stresses of daily life?

You might know the verse "Be still and know that I am God" (Psalm 46:10). However, the word translated as "Be still" is the same word that the prophet Samuel used when confronting King Saul for serious wrongdoing, when he failed to wait for the prophet to arrive and instead offered the sacrifices himself (1 Samuel 15:16). There, the word is translated as "Stop!" and "Enough!" These words give a much sharper and more striking tone to this verse: "Stop! And know that I am God" or "Enough! Know that I am God." In other words, be halted in your tracks, stop pretending that you are the one in control, busy with your own affairs; stop doing things your way and recognise that God is far greater, stronger, wiser and so on. Think on Him for a moment. Perhaps all of us, from time to time, need to hear that much louder command to stop rather than the gentler exhortation to simply "be still".

Often, we only reflect on what has gone wrong when we have pushed ourselves to the limit—when we are exhausted or burnt out and forced to stop. It would be much better if we paused earlier, or even better, if we made it a regular habit to pause.

Sometimes, to change our rhythm or find ways to remove major sources of stress, we need to make bold and radical choices, like switching jobs or careers. Most of the factors that inundate our lives are beyond our control or ability to change, such as family situations or global political issues. So, what can we do? How can we find peace and stillness amid such pressure?

"Be still and know that I am God" may offer us a clue. Psalm 46:10 is a frequently quoted scripture, and while that may seem like a wonderful hope, the practice can appear elusive or even impossible. However, a few verses earlier, the psalmist provides us with a helpful prompt. Verse 8 reads, "Come and see what the Lord has done." The psalmist seems to be encouraging us to divert our attention from distractions and deliberately focus on what God is doing. This is what will bring us peace—when we recognise that God is indeed God, and despite everything we may observe and struggle with, God remains in control. Verse 11 reassures us that "The Lord Almighty is with us, The God of Jacob is our fortress." When we are under assault from the world, whether it be general noise or our thoughts being deeply troubled by personal or global issues, a fortress sounds like an incredibly safe place to be. But how do we arrive there? How do we uncover this metaphoric fortress, this refuge of safety and peace?

The psalmist, while urging us to step away from our daily routines and distractions, commands us to "be still" or "stop". How exactly do we accomplish that? I don't know about you, but I find stillness very difficult. By nature, I am a doer. I cannot sit in a chair and do nothing, if I even manage to sit in the chair at all. I will either be scrolling through social media, crocheting or keeping my hands busy doing something else. Even reading is not a passive pastime; while our bodies are still, our minds are active and engaged with the text, whether it's a magazine, a substantial tome or a simple novel—our minds remain busy and occupied. I suspect only a very small minority of us can comfortably sit and do nothing. So why this command to be still? Fortunately for us, that is not the end of the sentence; we must connect it with the second part of the phrase: "and know that I am God."

Thankfully, it is not about sitting passively and doing nothing; it is about intentionally calming ourselves, not only from activity but from all other things that absorb our mental energy, deliberately seeking out and recognising God, taking the time to observe the works of His hands. For some, that may seem an enjoyable thing to do; for others, it might appear to be an incredible stretch. I hope that throughout this book, you will find helpful tips and guidance to assist you along the way.

Our bodies are truly remarkable. For instance, have you noticed how your brain has tuned out those background sounds you were listening to earlier? However, we need to look after our bodies and minds and eliminate distractions to our "listening". Like any precisely calibrated piece of equipment, our body, mind and spirit require careful balance and regular maintenance.

We all need time to reflect on our lives, the choices we have made and the journey we have travelled so far, to evaluate where we are and where we might be heading. We may ask ourselves and God, "Am I living in the fullness of life that Jesus has won for me?" Truly, it is not possible to reflect at this depth without intentionally taking time away from our daily hubbub. Perhaps you feel torn between the desire to be still and a persistent pull towards activity and that never-ending to-do list. Sadly, this is part of the human condition, and our reading of certain Bible texts in isolation may actually contribute to the confusion.

The Bible contains many seemingly paradoxical commands and statements—things we must carefully balance. Let's look at some of these.

Returning to the creation story in Genesis, we see a God who made us to be in relationship with one another from the very beginning (Genesis 2:18). He understood that we needed others around us to reach our full potential. He also intended for people to have a purpose (Genesis 1:28), which, after the fall, became a hardship (Genesis 3:17 – 19). In the New Testament, we are urged to "run with perseverance the race marked out for us" (Hebrews 12:1) and to "run in such a way to get the prize. Everyone who competes in the games goes into strict training" (1 Corinthians 9:24 – 25). Jesus Himself commanded us to "Go and make disciples of all nations" (Matthew 28:19), which seems like a rather immense task. Doing, doing, doing—busy, busy, busy—sounds familiar, doesn't it? Much of it is good and commendable work, striving hard in various activities—all effort for the kingdom. Or is it?

Alongside that, we must balance these other verses. Not only "Be still and know that I am God" but also "Whoever dwells in the shelter of the Most High will rest in the shadow of the Almighty" (Psalm 91:1). The Prophet Isaiah expressed these words, speaking on God's behalf: "My people will live in peaceful dwelling places, in secure homes, in undisturbed places of rest" (Isaiah 32:18); "Those who hope in [wait on] the Lord will renew their strength" (Isaiah 40:31). And Jesus Himself said, "Come to me, all you who are weary and burdened, and I will give you rest" (Matthew 11:28).

How can we reconcile this pressure to be active, to strive for our best, to make every effort to be productive, to care for those in need around us, to challenge social injustice and so on, with the expectation that we will also be people of rest? We will look at Mary and Martha in a later chapter, but their story captures the tensions we feel between what must be achieved and the deep longing in our souls to "be still". We must find a way to exist in both worlds, and God has clearly provided a path for us to live this way. We can be confident that He would not ask us to do something that is impossible.

Again, right at the beginning, God showed us the way. Whether we see the creation story as a literal six days or some other timeframe, the reality is that at the start, God rested on the seventh day. Adam, or mankind, was created on the sixth day, so Adam's very first experience of life was rest, not activity. He worked from a place of rest, resting with God. As an aside, while it is beyond our understanding, I wonder what God was doing before He created? Perhaps He was also resting.

This need for a balanced rhythm of life was further established when Moses received the Ten Commandments, the fourth being "Remember the Sabbath day by keeping it holy. Six days you shall labour and do all your work, but the seventh day is a sabbath to the Lord your God. On it you shall not do any work, neither you, nor your son or daughter, nor your male or female servant, nor your animals, nor any foreigner residing in your towns. For in six days the Lord made the heavens and the earth, the sea, and all that is in them, but he rested on the seventh day. Therefore, the Lord blessed the Sabbath day and made it holy" (Exodus 20:8 –11). I quote the commandment in full for a reason. Too often these days, we work hard from Monday to Friday, and the weekend becomes the time to catch up on all the domestic duties that need to be done: housework, shopping, laundry, as well as taking the kids to football, dance or other activities and helping them with their homework. Fitting all that into one day is difficult, and it often spills over into Sunday as well. Moreover, with the significant relaxation of Sunday trading laws in the UK during the 1980s, the ease of shopping for anything at any time and the increased requirement for many to work on Sundays, the long-held expectation of a day of rest, has been utterly undermined. If we are serious about finding a regular place of rest, we may need to reclaim some of what has been lost. Yes, we might manage to attend church, but for those on the worship team, the sound desk or the coffee or creche rota, it may scarcely feel like a time of rest and renewal.

I recall a time when I felt pulled in every direction by an overwhelming to-do list. One morning, I woke up with my mind racing, thinking about all I had to accomplish that day; note that I was not praying but was merely worried and anxious about what lay ahead. Wearily, I swung my feet off the bed, and before they touched the ground, I heard God speak to me. He said, "There are enough hours in this day to do everything that I require of you." It literally stopped me in my tracks. Of course! It's obvious— God will not ask us to do what we do not have the capacity to do; it was such a light bulb moment for me. It felt as if the pressure had immediately lifted, and I reassessed everything I thought I needed to do, discovering that much of it was unnecessary and not on God's agenda. I even found myself walking at a more leisurely pace and stopped to talk to people along the way. I can't say that I never felt pressured again, but that experience has made me much quicker to assess why I feel pressured.

Pressure is a constant feature of our world; pressure to succeed at work, to earn more, to own more and to do better and go further in all aspects of life. It is not a sustainable way to live.

In some ways, it is not surprising that mental health has become such a significant issue when we have lost the simple patterns and rhythms through which we were created to live. I understand that many factors contribute to this and that there are no easy solutions, but we are finely-tuned instruments that need careful balance. For the sake of our minds, souls and bodies, we must find these places of rest, where we focus on God and look beyond ourselves to see His works. For many of us, keeping Sundays free of commitments is not always possible, but it is crucial for our emotional and spiritual well-being to find other times to be still and pause.

The experience of the pandemic in 2020 and the observance of lockdown, with its hour of daily exercise, enabled many to (re)discover the joy of walking in the great outdoors, to take time to look at the trees, to hear the birds and to experience the gentle sway of the wind through the branches. For some people, this habit has persisted as they have come to appreciate the sense of enjoyment and well-being it brings. However, for many, it is now a regrettable loss, a distant memory. The opportunity simply to take an hour outside, to look and to wonder at creation, to be aware of the changing seasons—all of these things help us to see beyond ourselves and may be the simplest form of "being still" internally, even though our bodies may be moving. Just this week, I was heartened to hear a national TV presenter, broadcasting an item from the grounds and gardens of a stately home, who, as he wandered along the borders and through the woodland, ended his piece with "just being in this environment does your soul good." Yes, he hit the nail on the head!

How much more might we find to be 'good for our souls' if we consciously took time to focus on God, listen to Him and seek what He might choose to reveal? Intentionally setting aside other commitments to give Him our undivided attention should be part of our purpose if we aspire to live life to its fullest.

Questions to Ponder

Read Psalm 46 in full. In light of this first chapter, which aspects stand out to you particularly?

What are the noises, whether external or internal, that you would like to silence? How might this be achieved?

If life is meant to be a balance, do you favour busyness or stillness? What might need to shift?

Reflect on any positive experiences you had during the pandemic. Have they stayed with you, or are there things you would like to regain?

Group Study

Share how balanced your life feels. What things create pressure? Where do you find moments of stillness? Discuss whether any changes in rhythm are necessary. Do you work from a place of rest, or do you rest from your work?

MARGARET WOODING JONES

Chapter 2

What Is a Quiet Day and What Does It Mean to Be Intimate with God?

"Remain in me, as I also remain in you. No branch can bear fruit by itself; it must remain in the vine. Neither can you bear fruit unless you remain in me"
(John 15:4).

One way to find that deliberate time of quiet is to take a quiet day. Schedule it in your diary; decisively clear a minimum of a morning or afternoon, or better still both, in order to have a time for stillness and reflection. It can be a period spent alone and unstructured or alongside others in a more organised way. It doesn't just happen, no matter how good your intentions are, but will need to be an intentional choice to schedule it in your diary.

For those who have never experienced an organised Quiet Day, there is a risk of making assumptions that could be completely inaccurate. There are as many different types of organised Quiet Days as there are people who lead them. Different approaches will suit different personalities but, simply put, a Quiet Day is a time dedicated to focusing on God, giving our full attention to seeking and hearing the One who is our Creator and Redeemer, or simply coming before Him in silence and waiting for Him to speak. My approach in preparing to lead a Quiet Day involves prayerfully choosing a few verses of scripture or a very short passage and exploring themes from it. The Bible is, after all, the "God-breathed" (2 Timothy 3:16) and the inspired Word of God. God, through the Holy Spirit, inspired individuals to write His story and share their experiences of the Living God in a living relationship. It therefore seems the obvious starting point if we wish to focus on Him and listen to what He might have to say to us today. Others may very skillfully use inspired art, music and/or poetry to help people engage with this deeper level of listening.

I will discuss the practicalities of organising a day in a later chapter, but for me, a Quiet Day would typically start around 10 am and end around 3 pm. This period is usually divided into three sections with breaks for coffee, tea and lunch. I see these breaks as an opportunity to extend hospitality to attendees. The rest of the time is spent in silence. I will offer a brief introductory thought for each session and then let participants explore freely, finding their own quiet space and using the time as they see fit. While I suggest activities they might like to try, I also encourage taking the time needed. The resources at the end of this book mainly stem from days I have previously led.

For many people, the idea of being organised and being with others during such a personal and intimate encounter may feel completely alien. If that describes you, then the outlined resources could be a helpful focus, as they can be used individually and alone.

For several years, I led a mid-week congregation, taught on Alpha, and helped facilitate a recovery course that our church ran at the time. I was also a clergy spouse and mother to two young children while hosting various guests along the way. There was always plenty happening, and it would have been easy to be swept up in the busyness and excitement of a vibrant, growing church. However, I recognised the need for some breathing space, and I tried, once a month, to drive out into the countryside for a day to have time alone to reflect and pray. I would find somewhere quiet to sit and be, read my Bible or write in my journal. I'd love to tell you it was a wonderfully life-giving and focused time (which it may have been in part), but the truth is, sometimes I fell asleep, and other times I just daydreamed, coming home feeling frustrated and cross that I had somehow wasted my time. While the sleep may have been exactly what I needed, the daydreaming left me discontented with how I had spent the day. Using a guide or having materials to follow would have been extremely helpful, which is why I want to share these resources. Use them slowly and deliberately, reflecting on your own life and engaging with God as you can.

So let us think a bit more about the "what." What is happening, or what takes place? The opening verse of this chapter offers us some clues. For several years, I had the privilege of working with a large team of young international people from various countries around the world. For most of them, English was not their first language, so teaching them biblical studies was always a challenge. One particular day, I was teaching from John 15, about Jesus being the vine, us being the branches and the importance of abiding in Him. The Bible translation we used included the word "abide", which is unlikely to appear in basic English lessons. Despite my best efforts, I inevitably used the word "abide" several times, though it turned out to be rather unhelpful. I kept emphasising the importance of staying close to Jesus, listening to Him and seeking Him out. We discussed ways to achieve this, both in our daily routines and within the broader rhythms of our lives. I enjoy engaging with those I teach, and we had lively and insightful comments from the group that had gathered. At the end of the lesson, one of the young people approached me and asked, "What does the word 'abide' mean?" If only she had asked at the beginning of the class!

Learning to abide is essential for our growth and fulfilment. The dictionary definitions are intriguing: remain, stay close to, follow, observe or obey. Essentially, Jesus is urging us to live within and rest in His presence. It was a valuable lesson for me. Choosing to take a quiet day, whether alone in the countryside or with others, is a conscious and deliberate decision to give God time to renew or reaffirm our abiding faith and our ongoing dependence on Him. Certainly, there is much more to abiding in Jesus than just occasionally taking a quiet day; it must become part of a daily routine of prayer and Bible reading if we want to be fruitful. However, deliberately setting aside time can help to renew and refresh that daily practice.

I recall having an extraordinary and unexpected experience with God. I had gone for a walk with some friends in the Swiss Alps; this was not an organised retreat, just a walk with friends. We had set off well below the snowline and trekked through beautiful open pastures and forests. Suddenly, we arrived at a plateau surrounded by trees where deep snow still lay on the ground. My companions were very excited by the snow, and as we waded knee-deep in it, we stumbled upon a stunning mountain lake. It was vast and breathtaking, surrounded by high peaks, which, along with the blue sky, reflected in the water. It was one of those idyllic scenes that you might see on a poster or screensaver. My friends were eager to explore further, but I had had enough and agreed to stay seated on a rock while they continued walking. As they left me and their voices faded away, I became aware of an almost deafening silence, save for the wind gently rustling through the trees above me. I sat and absorbed the stunning beauty all around: the snow, the water, the mountains, the trees, the reflections. I then noticed that on one side of the lake, the water was ruffled by the breeze, distorting the reflection of the surrounding scenery, while across most of the lake, the water was perfectly still, creating a flawless mirror of the mountains above. In that moment, I heard God speak into my heart. He simply said, "The stiller the water, the greater the reflection. If you will be still with Me, the greater will be the reflection of my character in you." I have never forgotten those words, and I can still see the image of the lake as clearly as if it were a photograph despite it being nearly twenty years ago.

Being still with God, taking time to seek Him and intentionally being in His presence will change and transform us. This is what intimacy with God looks like; it rarely happens spontaneously. James 4:8 suggests that we need to make the first move: "Come near to God and he will come near to you." The reality, of course, is that God is always present. "Never will I leave you; never will I forsake you" (Hebrews 13:5). Psalm 139:7 asks, "Where can I go from your Spirit?" and the psalmist concludes that there is literally nowhere in heaven, or in space, or on earth where God's Spirit is not present. It is we who move away from a conscious acknowledgement of Him, not He from us; therefore, we must make the effort to draw near. He cannot ignore a heart that is hungry for more of Him.

And here is the joy: as we draw near to Him and He to us, as we take time to reflect on His Word and absorb its truth, just as a branch draws up sap from the tree and is nourished by it, so are we nourished by Him. The sap is life-giving and enables the tree (or the vine) to grow leaves, blossom and bear fruit, without which it would die. According to Jesus's words in John 15:4, we too need to be nourished by God in order to grow and be fruitful for our character to be shaped and formed more and more into the image of God.

And how does character shaping or fruit forming occur? As we sit in His presence, immersed in His words and receptive to the gentle whispering of the Holy Spirit, we may begin to feel conviction about something within us that is not right and does not align with how God created us to be. Perhaps the clearest example of this is found in Isaiah 6:1 – 8, where the Prophet Isaiah has a vision of being in God's presence. As he observes God's holiness, he is immediately convicted of his own unworthiness and sinfulness. Even as he confesses his sin, an angel cleanses Isaiah's lips with a burning coal. That may sound somewhat harsh, but we must remember it is a metaphorical act, part of his spiritual vision. The change in his heart, however, is instant, and he responds to God's call to go to the people.

We may or may not be fortunate enough to experience such profound visions, but God always seeks to refine us and move us forward, transforming us, step by step, to become more like Him. God is incredibly gentle and compassionate, dealing with us so graciously that it is not something to fear; rather, it offers us an opportunity to surrender ourselves.

Perhaps the reason some of us are so reluctant to prioritise this quiet space is fear. We may be afraid of what God might say to us. We might experience a deep sense of guilt or self-condemnation for past wrongs or ongoing habitual sins or simply feel unworthy to approach Him. We could believe we have waited too long, thinking that God wouldn't want to draw near to us—everyone else, yes, but not ourselves. A sense of self-condemnation can be a huge obstacle to overcome.

The truth is that we often condemn ourselves, dismissing our worthiness because of feelings of shame. Yet, the Bible is filled with stories of God using people who didn't have perfect track records. Moses was a murderer hiding out in the desert, yet God met with him and called him to undertake the most incredible leadership journey ever told. King David was both a murderer and adulterer, but after being convicted (not condemned) by God with the guidance of the prophet Nathan, he went on to write some of the most beautiful psalms and to lead God's people into his old age. Indeed, he was named by God as "a man after his [God's] own heart" (1 Samuel 13:14). Psalm 51 is his confession and prayer to God; if you are struggling with similar feelings of unworthiness, you may wish to use this psalm to articulate your thoughts and feelings.

We might think of the Apostle Peter, who, having been a loyal follower and friend of Jesus, denied knowing Him completely when faced with pressure. What a miserable failure he must have felt! And yet in John 21:15 – 19, Jesus meets with him, restores him and commissions him for a life of service. A truly wonderful act of redemption.

There are many examples of individuals being radically changed by their encounters with Jesus. Zacchaeus was hated and despised by his own people, but one encounter transformed his heart forever. Mary Magdalene, a deeply troubled young woman, was transformed by her encounter with Jesus and became a devoted follower and worshipper of Him. I could go on! No wrongdoing is too deep or too grave for which Jesus has not already paid the price.

As we revisit the image of Jesus as the vine and ourselves as the branches, we are reminded that the Father is the Gardener who will cut off every branch in us that does not bear fruit and prune those that do. While the idea of being cut or even pruned may sound painful, let us consider this for a moment. If there is some aspect of our lives—something that takes our time and attention and is not fruitful or serves no useful purpose—wouldn't you want to be rid of it so you can dedicate your time and focus on something that will have a lasting impact? Being quiet before God allows Him, and us, to have that conversation and to submit ourselves anew to His guidance. It seems like a win/win situation to me. (See also Resource 9.)

Difficult questions about our attitudes or behaviour can be challenging to address, but they become much easier when we pause, sit down and have a genuine heart-to-heart with God. Many of us try to tackle the big questions of life while juggling the pressures of daily responsibilities. It's somewhat like conversing with someone while both are preoccupied with other tasks; you might be half-listening, yet your focus is diverted elsewhere. You may not see their face, expressions or body language, which often results in miscommunication, leading to misunderstandings or half-heard messages. The same applies to our relationship with God. It is truly remarkable that we can reach out to Him wherever and whenever we choose. Nonetheless, we must consciously give Him our undivided attention, just as my husband and I do when we have something significant to discuss. We sit down and offer each other our full attention; it is the same with God. We rarely hear Him when we neglect to devote our attention to Him.

Sometimes God captures our attention; perhaps even picking up this book has been part of that process. I mentioned Moses earlier, so let's return to him for a moment. There he was, in the desert, hiding in fear for his life. You can read the full story in Exodus 2 and 3. Having lived in the Egyptian palace, separated from his family and his people and after murdering an Egyptian slave driver out of anger at the injustices he witnessed, his life was in danger; Pharaoh sought to kill him. Having known all the wealth and splendour of court life, Moses had become the lowest of the low—a shepherd wandering the desert, forging a meagre existence for years. If anyone felt excluded or disqualified, it might have been him. Yet, it is in that very situation that God captures his attention, and he has a life-changing encounter as God shares His own heart with Moses.

I wonder what God might be waiting to share with you if He could simply hold your attention for longer than a few minutes?

Questions to Ponder

If you have never participated in a formal Quiet Day or spent an extended period in silence to listen to God, what are your concerns? What could help you overcome those barriers?

If you feel disqualified or unworthy, how do the stories of Moses, Peter or Mary Magdalene inspire you?

Take your time to read Psalm 51 slowly and thoughtfully. Then read it again. Which verse or verses catch your attention? What might the Lord be trying to show or say to you through these verses?

Group Study

If anyone has attended an organised Quiet Day, share how you felt beforehand and how your fears were eased.

Share any moments when God has "caught your attention". What happened, and how did you change?

Share together your own practices of abiding in Jesus.

Chapter 3

Who Might Benefit from a Quiet Day?

"As the deer pants for streams of water, so my soul pants for you, my God" (Psalm 42:1).

This brief verse from Psalm 42 offers a powerful visual of the psalmist's desperation for God's presence. Few of us have ever experienced extreme thirst, but this image of a deer, possibly pursued or hunted and panting desperately for water, sparks our imagination. For the psalmist, it symbolises the deep longing of his heart to seek intimacy with God. He feels that this heartfelt longing would be fulfilled if only he could draw near to God and spend time in His presence. Have you ever felt that same profound longing or experienced disappointment when that yearning remains unfulfilled?

The mathematician and physicist Blaise Pascal is famously quoted as referring to a God-shaped hole in each of us, but what he actually said is more profound and presents a far more powerful image. He stated, "There is a God-shaped vacuum in the heart of each man which cannot be satisfied by any created thing but only by God the Creator, made known through Jesus Christ."

A hole indicates a space or void, but a vacuum is more active and forceful, suggesting a deficit—a space that, once opened, will be instantly filled. Have you ever struggled with a vacuum-packed duvet or mattress? Once it is removed from the vacuum and filled with air, it will never return to the tiny bag in which it was delivered. What a picture of our hearts! Once we open our hearts to Him, there is an immediate change—a filling, a restoration that can only be completed and occupied by God Himself, the very One who made us, crafted us and knows us intimately. It is God alone who can fill and satisfy that longing. Jesus Christ Himself came to this world to help us understand more about who God is and how we can relate to Him through the presence and power of the Holy Spirit.

I remember a time in my life when, despite witnessing God's powerful movement in our church community and seeing many come to faith and be transformed, a deep cry within me was, "There has to be more than this!" I am sure many longed to see what we were experiencing then, and wanting more might seem almost greedy or ungrateful. However, deep down in my soul, there was such a profound longing that what we were experiencing felt almost peripheral to the place God truly wanted to occupy within me. I recall asking someone to pray that I would "know God deep in my guts." I lacked the words to express the depth of my longing.

I believe that each of us, if we could simply allow a little time and space to reflect on our inner thoughts or the needs of our souls, would uncover that same dissatisfaction, that desperate thirst or hunger for more. It is easy to disguise it, to immerse ourselves in other pursuits or to postpone it for a more convenient time (which, by the way, will never arrive). We have already discussed the busyness of life, but if we are to be truly whole and healthy, living in the fullness of life (John 10:10) that Christ has won for us, we cannot achieve this without continually drawing close to the One who created us and who sustains us day by day.

We have mentioned the importance of daily quiet moments, reading the Bible and communing with God, but that may be more like taking a few sips of water rather than a long, thirst-quenching drink.

Each of us needs to deliberately and intentionally take more time to simply be present with God in order to satisfy that longing.

For some, the idea of silence can be frightening. I remember a time many years ago, before most people had mobile phones, when I taught a group of young interns about the importance of quietly meditating on scripture. Partway through the session, I announced that we would spend the next 30 minutes alone, in silence, to meditate on a specific passage. I asked those with phones to switch them off. I was caught off guard by a barrage of questions from the group, with the most common being "Can I listen to music?" and "What if God doesn't speak?" There was also a genuine sense of horror at the thought of not speaking for a full 30 minutes! I encouraged them as best I could to sit with the passage of scripture, reread it if their minds wandered and actively listen to what God might want to say to them. To say they were sceptical, wary and a little fearful would be an understatement. Yet, 30 minutes later, they all returned, most in disbelief that the time had already passed. Everyone, without exception, had gained something truly positive from the experience, and each was eager to share the insights God had revealed or something else that had caught their attention during their pause to reflect, discovering that God had spoken into their lives. My prayer was that these young interns would experience enough of this to make it a regular part of their discipleship.

I suspect that nowadays, every generation, not just the young, might struggle to give up contact with their phones for any length of time let alone four or five hours during an organised Quiet Day. When I lead Quiet Days, I often observe people checking their phones during coffee or lunch breaks. I am sure some genuinely need to check on childcare arrangements and similar matters, but many are clearly just scrolling through social media, which creates a constant distraction and detracts from our spiritual focus.

For some, the concept of silence is a delight and something to seek out while for others, it is daunting and something to avoid at all costs. Let us consider these two extremes briefly and explore how personality type might shape these views.

There are those who truly enjoy the idea of peace, quiet and space just to "be". Generally, one might say that introverts—who often feel drained by interactions with others—value the chance for stillness and tranquillity; however, this is not necessarily the case when we specifically discuss creating space for God. They may also feel some anxiety but could be more willing to try it. It is true that introverts might actually be less inclined to sign up for an organised Quiet Day, where there is a risk of others interrupting their experience. They might prefer to retreat entirely by themselves to seek God alone.

Once again, we can generalise and state that extroverts, those who thrive on human interaction, are more likely to struggle with knowing how to handle silence and may actively avoid booking a quiet day. Both of these are broad generalisations, and one might ask, "So who does come on a Quiet Day?" From my experience, it is people willing to give it a try and who have found that extroverts can remain quiet, especially when given guidance on how to spend the time, alongside introverts who appreciate meeting others with a shared aim: to spend time with God.

A friend shared, "Two ways I find help to be quiet with God are the thought-provoking and often challenging mini-talks and the follow-up questions for each part of the day. With my ADHD brain, I feel I can't manage it without that stimulation. That means a lot to me. I feel unable to simply '"be quiet with God with an empty mind!" I believe another character distinction is relevant, and that is between the "be-ers" and the "do-ers". Those who find stillness easy and it comes naturally to them, and those who, by nature, are busy—who cannot bear to sit down without having something "to do", who feel they need to engage in something productive and who cannot endure if they perceive themselves as wasting time.

I've spent a significant amount of time examining the story of Mary and Martha, as found in Luke 10:38 – 42. It is a well-known story, one that people often quote, especially when they are overly busy. Poor Martha gets very bad press! From reading the story, we get the impression that Mary simply wanted to spend time with Jesus, listening to His every word, and that time and responsibilities were ignored, while Martha is portrayed as the unfortunate one who had to do all the work. But have you ever noticed that it was actually Martha who invited Jesus into the house? (Luke 10:38). It was Martha who opened her home to Him, Martha who desired His presence with them and, in doing so, wanted to offer the very best in hospitality. We must also remember that it wasn't just Jesus who came but also His disciples. There would likely have been quite a crowd to feed, so it is not surprising that Martha had a lot on her mind.

As Jesus spoke and Mary listened, it seemed that Martha became resentful and expressed her feelings to Jesus, "Don't you care that I've been left to do the work by myself?" I wonder how many of us have echoed a similar sentiment? "A quiet day? Yes, I'd love one, but the Toddler Group won't run itself... someone has to do the shopping...bring in a salary...."

Fill in the blanks for yourself. All these tasks are good and important, but—and it's a significant but—Jesus points out that Mary had made listening to Him a priority, and it wouldn't be taken away from her. He does not say that what Martha was doing was bad or unnecessary but that Mary had chosen the better thing. And while it is not written in scripture, I can't help but think that, knowing Jesus's character and His freedom from conforming to the social norms of the day, if she too had sat and listened, He and His disciples would all have joined in to help prepare the meal and set the table, and they probably would have enjoyed much fun in the process!

Being a "do-er", an activist, engrossed in or overwhelmed by responsibilities, however good and worthy they may be, cannot serve as an excuse for not taking the time to be still with Jesus. I have witnessed time and again that individuals who have sacrificially made time to be with Jesus find that their burdensome workload has lightened. They "somehow" managed to accomplish more work in less time, or someone else unexpectedly stepped up to fill the gap. When we prioritise time for Jesus, He will not see us depleted or failing; in fact, quite the opposite.

While it can be challenging for those who work full-time and have other weekend responsibilities to find the time to take a break, it can also be difficult for individuals in full-time Christian ministry to give themselves permission to take time off. I was surprised when, at a recent conference for church leaders, I attended a seminar entitled "Becoming Holier, Healthier and Humble Leaders". As the session began, attendees were invited to use an app to anonymously respond to the question, "What question would you not want to be asked?" Given that most attendees were either ordained leaders or individuals with significant leadership roles in their local churches, it was sad to see the most common response. Time and again, the message "Please don't ask me about my prayer life/spiritual life" appeared on the screen via the app. How can it be that the church and its associated activities impose such demands on our leaders that they cannot find time to prioritise prayer? Quiet days are not just for church leaders, but it is essential that they have the freedom and permission to be still and attend to their own spiritual well-being. Failing to do so could ultimately have a devastating effect on both themselves and the church they serve.

Another character difference worth noting is the contrast between those who value structure and those who prize freedom. With the Quiet Days I facilitate, I aim to offer opportunities for both. While I provide brief input during each of the (usually) three sessions, 45 minutes to an hour are set aside for silent reflection. I offer optional pointers on how to use that time, which many find especially helpful to stay focused; however, others prefer to follow their own path. Once again, different personalities react in different ways. There are no strict rules about what must be done. I have a dear friend who is also involved in church leadership and often attends my Quiet Days. She wrote this: "The very idea of taking time out of an extremely busy day to spend meaningful time with God attracted me from the first time I received your invitation to attend one. Since that day, I have always seized the opportunity to participate in your Quiet Days and often tell people that my favourite comment is, 'They are better than a spa day!'"

Many people probably struggle with how to handle a long period of quiet without some structure to guide them; this book was therefore created. If the thought of being with others is unappealing for your encounter with God but the emptiness of unstructured time is also a difficulty, then the resources in this book might be exactly what you need to stay focused, whether you decide to sit in a park, a coffee shop or, like me, simply drive out to a remote place.

For those who live alone, the thought of even more silence might feel daunting. Why retreat to a quiet place when I already experience silence all day, every day? However, taking a break from routine and spending time with others who share the same goal can help one to hear God. A widowed friend who lives alone wrote, "I have found quiet days away help me spend time with God in a way that is not so easy at home, where there are other distractions. They encourage me to study His Word and sit quietly with Him as He teaches me. My faith is strengthened by having meaningful time with God. To prioritise time for a quiet day, I need to block out other engagements so I can focus wholly on Him. The most helpful atmosphere is to be in a different place from my home or church, where I might be easily distracted from thoughts of God."

We often tend to put people in boxes or categorise their spirituality, and there is a risk that we may dismiss different practices as not "fitting" our theological framework or experience. This can lead to a kind of "that's not how we do things here" attitude. Quiet Days might fit into that box; you may not know anyone else who has attended one, or you might imagine that they are for the super-spiritual or those from a different churchmanship. In his helpful book, 'Sacred Pathways', Gary Thomas describes nine distinct spiritual temperaments, each with its own preferences for connecting with God, ranging from contemplatives to activists. However, he prefaces all of the descriptors by stating that regardless of someone's spiritual temperament, everyone needs to find that place of stillness and silence.

My background is perhaps a little unusual. I came to faith as a teenager in a moderate, liturgical Anglican church that was also experiencing the charismatic renewal in the mid-1970s. For me, a sung Eucharist was deeply moving and remains something I enjoy from time to time. However, alongside that, the freedom and joy of charismatic worship were equally familiar to me at the time. Throughout my Christian journey, I have had the privilege of worshipping in various denominations, traditions and styles. In the late 1990s, I visited the Toronto Vineyard Church, home of what was known as the Toronto Blessing, which was both wild and exhilarating. That same year, I also experienced my first silent retreat in an abbey in Oxfordshire, involving three days of complete silence, apart from about 20 minutes with a nun on the first day. The contrast could not have been greater, and yet both experiences profoundly impacted and enriched my life, as both places provided significant encounters with God for me.

We truly are "fearfully and wonderfully made" (Psalm 139:14). We are complex beings, and although we may have our preferred ways of doing things, it is often a fear of stepping outside our norm that stops us from experiencing other opportunities. When I trained to be a licensed lay minister, the course leader required me to undertake a placement in a church tradition with which I had no prior experience. To be honest, that didn't leave many options; the only thing left on the list was a very high Anglican church with all its ritual and sense of ceremony. I was quite nervous about what to expect. I need not have worried. I discovered a reverence and awe of God that was beautiful, and although I might not have been completely at ease with everything theologically, I still had a profound experience of God in that place and among the people there. We cannot and must not put things in boxes; if we want to experience the fullness of life, then let's step out of our comfort zones and try something different. If you have never experienced a Quiet Day or a longer retreat, consider booking one soon. Periods of stillness set aside to listen to God are essential for everyone regardless of character type or personal preferences. How you choose to engage in this practice is entirely up to you, whether it involves walking alone in the hills or joining others on a retreat or Quiet Day. My prayer is that, if it is not already, it becomes a practice that enriches your life.

Questions to Ponder

Do you ever feel a deep longing within your soul to draw closer to God?

Are you by nature a Mary or a Martha? Carefully reread Luke 10:38 – 42 several times and ask God what He would reveal to you about Himself and yourself.

Have you ever been tempted to dismiss quiet days as something only "super-spiritual people" engage in?

Group Study

Could you share your personal experiences of trying to be quiet with God? How easy or challenging do you find it? What things have been helpful? How much do your responses mirror the different personalities within the group?

Chapter 4

How to Use a Quiet Day. How Might We Hear God's Voice and How Do We Avoid Distractions?

"The Lord is my shepherd, I lack nothing. He makes me lie down in green pastures, he leads me beside quiet waters, he refreshes my soul"

(Psalms 23:1 –3).

These words are among the most well-known Bible verses, certainly within the Christian community and possibly also in the wider community. They form part of the liturgy and are often sung at both wedding and funeral services. We may fully agree with them as truth, but I wonder whether we live them out, practise them or truly experience them in our lives?

If a sheep lies down, it can do little else. What it is most likely doing is chewing the cud, which means regurgitating and re-chewing food previously consumed. They then re-swallow it to extract every bit of goodness from the lush green grass they have been feeding on. This process occurs primarily when the animal is at rest. Apparently, healthy mature sheep will chew the cud for several hours a day. While regurgitation may not sound particularly glamorous, it serves as a powerful illustration for us of truly meditating on God's Word, our spiritual food, extracting every bit of goodness from it that we can. Can you imagine the pleasure of simply lying down and savouring a verse or two of scripture, uncovering every nugget of truth hidden within it?

Here once again is the picture of still waters, a safe and tranquil place to drink, a calm location to satisfy that thirst—perhaps a gently flowing brook of clear water—because bodies of completely still water with no inflow or outflow tend to be stagnant and unpleasant. The image evokes peace and calm, not a dangerously raging torrent. If you have ever seen sheep or other animals drinking from a pool or brook, you will notice that it isn't all entirely beautiful and idyllic. The animals, in the very act of reaching the water, stir up the mud and create a complete mess.

Again, how true is that to our own image? We often stir up muck and mess as we come to God. Our pain, anger or sheer brokenness block the way; arguments, accusations or sorrowful thoughts muddy the waters as we approach. Yet, it is these very things that God longs to wash away and cleanse from us, just as the gently flowing stream washes away the mud and sediment stirred up by the animals. Every time we come to drink from the Word, a little more of our mess is washed away and a little more of His character is revealed within us. Just as gently as the waters wash around the sheep's hooves, so gently does He deal with us. God is not out with a sharp scrubbing brush, desperately trying to remove deep stains; no, He comes gently, washing over us with His love and grace, so softly that it's almost imperceptible. That's not to say that He doesn't challenge us to change our behaviour or to take a different path. Still, it is always an invitation, not a command, often driven by our love for Him and our desire to follow Him more closely. What may have once seemed challenging actually becomes the obvious choice for us.

It is also important to note that the psalmist is very realistic about life's hardships and difficulties; there is nothing sugar-coated here. Further in the psalm, we read of the "darkest valley" (Psalm 23:4), which could not be more graphic. We have all experienced this, whether through the loss of beloved friends or family or through our own sickness, trauma, pain or fears. He is honest about the reality of facing enemies, which come in all shapes and sizes, both internal and external. It is amid these hardships of life that God leads us and offers us not just sustenance—enough to get by—but an actual feast. The question is, will we partake of the feast? Will we allow ourselves to be led into the green pastures and by the still waters to which He guides us?

I realise I have written a lot about "encountering God" and "hearing God's voice", and you might be curious about what that truly looks and sounds like. There are many ways in which God may speak to us, and the topic probably deserves a whole book on its own.

One of the main ways God speaks to us is through the pages of scripture. This is why we benefit from reading a passage more than once, whether during our daily time of prayer and quiet or in a longer session. There is a risk that we might quickly skim scripture and, almost metaphorically, give God a smiley face emoji when we encounter a verse we like before moving on to the next thing. Perhaps we even copy and paste it onto our favourite platform so others can appreciate it too, where it will undoubtedly receive a smiley face or heart emoji. If we want to gain the fullest benefit from the Word, we must approach it with reverence and the expectation that it will profoundly nourish us. Please note I am not suggesting that posting scripture online is trivial; it can be incredibly timely and meaningful.

The practice of reading, rereading and continually engaging with the same few verses can help us notice details, such as a word or phrase that suddenly seems to gain particular significance that we hadn't observed on the first reading. This is what it means to meditate on scripture or engage in the practice of Lectio Divina, a form of divine reading. On first reading, there may be an intellectual connection, a memory of having heard this verse before (or not, as the case may be) or an acknowledgement that this is a truth. However, repeated reading begins to shift from being solely in our heads to engaging our hearts or souls. It is challenging to describe how that transition occurs; all I can suggest is that you try it yourself. You may have noticed that in the question sections at the end of each chapter, this practice has been recommended as an activity, so hopefully, you have started to experience something of this practice already. Bible meditation, or Lectio Divina, sounds much more appealing than regurgitation or chewing the cud, but essentially, that is what it is!

As we read scripture for reflection, it is important to recognise that we are not engaging in a traditional Bible study, where one might seek to understand the source and context of the passage, possibly comparing different versions and examining background or related texts. We are not approaching scripture to ask questions but to listen—to listen to the words of the text, to read, reread and again reread. And then to sit and listen.

As you read, simply sit and listen. It is so easy for us to want to launch into prayer, whether for ourselves or for others. We read words that we believe might be helpful for someone else, and so we stray off on a tangent and pray for them. I have a preacher friend who refers to this as the snowplough effect, where we perceptively discern, whether rightly or wrongly, what someone else might need but forget to listen to the Word for ourselves.

As you sit with scripture and listen, which particular word or phrase resonates deeply with you or comes more strongly to your conscious attention? Sit with those words; what is the Lord saying to you? What is He showing you? Is He bringing to mind some long-forgotten memory? If so, ask Him why. What is its relevance to today and this moment?

The scripture before you might reveal a new or different aspect of His character, guiding you deeper into worship and awe. Reflect on it and let your heart be moved by that insight. How might you express that? Writing, drawing, singing?

Perhaps God gently brings to mind something more painful or a situation that you have been struggling with. It may be that He, in His love and compassion towards you, knows that you cannot move forward in your life without first allowing Him to touch you and bring healing to your heart. Allow yourself to be touched by Him, and if tears flow, let them. As we have considered previously, God does not bring up difficult things to condemn us but to gently convict and help us reach a place of greater freedom, enabling us to let go of difficulties by bringing them to the cross of Jesus, leaving them there and entrusting them to His judgement and care.

If you are genuinely seeking guidance in decision-making, you may find that the words before you offer another piece in the process, even if they do not provide the full answer. These elements must be considered in the context of other words, experiences and preferably, with the counsel of a minister or wise friends.

You might feel afraid that you won't hear God's voice or recognise it when you do. You are not alone in this, but as you try to quiet your thoughts, seek Him, read His Word or even marvel at the beauty of creation around you, you may hear His gentle whisper deep within. If you remain unsure, then ask the question, "Lord, what would you say to me?" Other helpful ways to approach Bible meditation include asking the question, "What did that actually look like?" Try to visualise the scene: who was there? What might the bystanders have been doing or saying? What might have been their reaction? What was the tone of voice of the speaker or speakers? Visiting the Holy Land some years ago completely transformed my reading of scripture, as I could suddenly visualise the landscape. I could almost feel the heat of the sun on the roadway or picture the beauty of the Galilean hills. 'The Chosen', a dramatization of the Gospel accounts of Jesus's life, available on Amazon Prime, provides helpful insight into the kind of background and normal, everyday life into which Jesus entered. Visualisation can be a powerful tool.

For some, another question to consider might be, "Who am I in this story?" This is especially helpful when we read some of the parables. "If I were standing in front of Jesus as He said this, what would have been my response? What is my response now?"

Another way that God speaks to me and many others is visually. In the book of the prophet Habakkuk, there is an interesting little verse that says, "I will stand at my watch and station myself on the ramparts; I will look to see what he will say to me" (Habakkuk 2:1). That may sound rather strange; normally, we would expect to see with our eyes and hear with our ears. However, if you think about it, although studies vary, the consensus is that around 55% of how we communicate when we are present in person is through observed body language (and only around 7% through actual words, the remainder being through tone of voice). That's staggering; more than half of what we are "hearing" when we listen to someone is actually from what we are seeing visually. We process so much through observation, so why would it not be the same in our communication with God?

It can rightly be argued that, since we cannot see God directly, observing His body language is impossible. God is omnipresent; as we have already noted, He is everywhere, both within us and outside of us. There is nowhere He is not, but even so, we are not currently interacting with or viewing a physical body. Nonetheless, we are part of and living within His beautiful creation, which David describes so beautifully in Psalm 19:1–4: "The heavens declare the glory of God; the skies proclaim the work of his hands. Day after day they pour forth speech; night after night they reveal knowledge. They have no speech, they use no words; no sound is heard from them. Yet their voice goes out into all the earth, their words to the ends of the world."

Everything around us literally speaks of Him, and as it does, He can speak to our hearts through these surroundings. I love how Jesus, as He looked around, used whatever He saw to convey a spiritual truth or lesson. We have already considered Jesus as the vine and us as the branches. I imagine that He was walking through a vineyard or past a vine as He spoke those words. The parables were all illustrative stories from everyday life—a farmer sowing his crops, lost coins, mustard seeds, wedding banquets, fig trees, housebuilding; the list goes on. Why would God not speak to us through what we see and observe? There have been many times when God has drawn my attention through the things around me: a tall poplar tree swaying in the breeze, a flower, a rocky headland, the reflection in a lake; to be honest, the list is endless. What we truly need is the desire or expectation, coupled with an inner attentiveness to what He might say.

When I was on my silent retreat in Oxfordshire, I wandered around the garden, not contemplating any profound spiritual thoughts. Instead, I was reflecting on my current sense of confusion about my own identity. As a young, sleep-deprived, stay-at-home mother, much of life seemed to revolve around nappies, washing and baby talk. I no longer had the responsible job I had once loved, and my confidence had plummeted over the years that followed. As I walked along, I suddenly noticed the tiniest fly on a leaf. Sitting in the sun, its little body radiated every iridescent colour of the rainbow. It was utterly beautiful, a most incredible work of art. I stood there for a while, marvelling that something so tiny could be so captivatingly beautiful. As I gazed, I heard God whisper to me something along the lines of, "I took great care in creating that tiny fly, and it is perfect. How much more care have I taken in creating you? You, too, are part of my perfect creation, and I love you." My gaze shifted away from myself and was firmly directed towards God. I later learned from one of the nuns that this particular species of fly was very rare, yet it seemed to thrive within the abbey grounds. Some may still wonder, how do we actually hear Him? Again, this is hard to describe, and the experience may differ for different people. Personally, it feels a bit like a thought that comes to mind; it's quiet but persistent yet not forceful. Sometimes it appears as a kind of mental picture. It's very easy to miss or overlook if we are busy with other things. A friend once described it as "knowing in your know-er". Elijah described it well in 1 Kings 19:12 as the "gentle whisper".

1 Kings 19:9 –14 is a fascinating story about how we might hear God's voice. It begins with the weary prophet Elijah hiding in a cave and having a conversation with God. God asks him why he is there, and Elijah responds by pouring out his heart in complaint to God. "Complaint" may be an understatement; I think he was probably raging! Then the Lord instructs Elijah to go and stand at the mouth of the cave because He is about to pass by. Firstly, Elijah witnesses a mighty wind that brings the rocks crashing down; then there is an earthquake that shakes the very ground he stands on and finally, there is a fire. It must have been terrifying! Yet each time it says God was not in...the wind/earthquake/fire.

What was Elijah expecting? What do we expect when God speaks? The truly interesting aspect of this account is that God speaks to Elijah in exactly the same way after all the devastating natural disasters as He did beforehand. In the same quiet manner, He asks precisely the same question: "What are you doing here Elijah?" What's even more intriguing is that Elijah responds in exactly the same way too! It made me wonder how many times we have repeated conversations with God.

There have been moments in life when I have cried out, asking God to make an answer clear, especially regarding direction in life choices. Together with others, I have asked that God just write on the wall and make it obvious. However, we might need to examine that particular Bible story more closely to realise that we probably don't want God to use that method, no matter how helpful it might seem at the time. The entire account is found in Daniel 5, which shows extreme debauchery, arrogance and godlessness. The words written on the wall were a message of severe judgement against King Belshazzar and perhaps the only way God could have got his attention in such an environment of drunkenness, feasting and excess. If we are asking, "God, what are you saying? Show me which way to go," then God certainly will not need to get our attention in the same manner because He already has it.

For many, if not all, distraction is a very real problem and a struggle for those who aim to set aside time for God. Thoughts about work or household matters suddenly come to the forefront of the mind, or the need to remember to buy washing-up liquid seems to take on an urgency that is wholly disproportionate. For some, the tendency to daydream, fall down a rabbit hole or simply get lost in thought can lead to significant frustration, especially when time feels so precious. There are several practical steps we can take to help counteract such distractions. First, minimise distractions as much as possible. Make sure nothing requires your immediate or urgent attention, whether in person or via email. Set your out-of-office reply so that others won't bother you for a response. Turn off your phone, or better still, keep it out of reach entirely. If you're using a laptop or tablet to read your Bible or journal, disable all notifications. Yes, you read correctly: switch them off.

If something comes to mind that you don't want to forget (like the shopping list or an errand), take a moment to jot it down, preferably on paper rather than your phone, as the risk is that you might then get distracted by your phone and end up down a different rabbit hole.

Sometimes our thoughts can be quite persistent: replaying a conversation that caused distress, considering how a different response could have changed the outcome or, as I must admit to having done once, engaging in a full-scale argument in my head. Perhaps it's revisiting an unhelpful image in your mind's eye. All of these distractions are harder to minimise. Instead of trying to erase them or run away from them, the safest approach is to take them to God. Be honest with Him about your feelings, frustrations and disappointments. Recognise that He knows every side of the story and understands your hurt and pain. Lay before Him whatever it is and observe how He responds to your honesty.

I remember a friend sharing with me that she had a completely irrational dislike for someone. Simply put, she just didn't like them; everything about them annoyed her, and her dislike was evident in her behaviour. She recalls being challenged by the group leader to change her ways, but try as she might, she just couldn't. Even as a very young Christian, she knew that this wasn't right, and in the end, she simply prayed, "Lord, you know I don't like her and I don't have it in me to love her. Please give me some of Your love because you have lots to spare." And that is precisely what He did. She suddenly found herself being kind to them, and her whole attitude towards them changed. Sometimes we need to admit our inability to do something and ask God to grant us some of His power to change.

Generally, these interactions with God take place in that quiet, solitary place with Him. While we all benefit from the connections made within community, meeting with and encouraging one another in our walk with God, such personal and intimate heart restoration typically happens as we submit ourselves alone to God.

Another source of distraction that can be difficult to ignore is those people for whom we feel a particular responsibility, whether that be a child, an elderly parent or a sick spouse. These responsibilities can be constant and intrusive, even when, or perhaps especially when, we are apart from them. It is helpful to remember that God cares for each person even more than we do, entrusting them to His care for the day. It may also be beneficial to pray that God will bless them in new and unexpected ways during your absence so that your mind and heart can be free from the burden and anxiety. Doing so may allow you to give your attention more fully to God for a few brief hours. It may be helpful to simply say out loud, "Father, into your loving hands, I place...." Then, proceed to the day's purpose.

Linked to that may be the false sense of responsibility we sometimes feel for others, such as a friend we've invited to join the Quiet Day. At times, we might believe that how they perceive the day reflects on us, especially if they are unhappy or criticise something that has been said or done. We need to let go of that idea and recognise that each person's response is their own responsibility.

So, whatever distractions you encounter that pull you away from single-minded devotion, be honest with yourself and with God. Take the practical steps you can, and talk to God about what you cannot change or let go.

Many of us find it difficult to read, pray and ponder without losing focus, so a very helpful tool could be to write or journal, whether that involves simply jotting down notes or more detailed entries. For some, seeing the words on the page helps their communication flow. For others, drawing, painting or simply doodling might assist, but care must be taken to ensure it doesn't become an end in itself, creating its own distraction. Others find it useful to use an object as a focus, whether a cross, a candle or an icon. If you have an organised day, your group leader may suggest using an object provided that relates to the theme of the day. In her book, 'The Ambassador,' Mandy Carr expands on the idea of journaling not just as a way for us to write our thoughts and reflections on the scripture we meditate on but also to listen and actively write, as if capturing God's side of the conversation. Since discovering this concept, I have tried it myself and been quite amazed by what has filled the pages of my journal; more importantly, it has also kept me remarkably focused.

Visio Divina, literally translated as "sacred seeing", is the practice of using art—usually a visual interpretation of a biblical scene or an icon—for the purpose of meditation. While this may serve as a helpful additional focus, it is not the primary emphasis of this book. Much else has been written about this form of Christian meditation.

Similarly, music may or may not help in maintaining focus. Some attendees of my Quiet Days have enjoyed soft, background worship music while others have certainly not. We must be cautious that the music itself does not become the central focus of our thoughts, though that's not to suggest, of course, that God cannot speak through music as well.

Another possible distraction could be our physical body. If you feel uncomfortable, too hot or too cold, it can be hard to stay focused. This might make you wish for the session to end so you can find a radiator or a hot drink. I always recommend wearing loose, comfortable clothes with plenty of layers. If you are sitting for a while, you don't want to feel cold or constantly be aware that your trousers are too tight. If you're going out alone, even on a day you've chosen to fast, I recommend taking a hot drink in a flask, even if it's just hot water. If you're participating in an organised day, check whether drinks and food are provided or if you need to take a packed lunch. It can really disrupt the flow of the day if you have to leave to buy sandwiches halfway through.

I've spoken about sitting all day, but it might be helpful to also consider posture. While sitting may be the most obvious position, depending on your surroundings, you might choose to lie face down or kneel as an outward sign of humility and reverence. You may, like Moses, feel the need to take off your shoes or perform some other physical act of reverence. When I lead a Quiet Day, I try, whenever possible, to provide enough space for people to be alone during the times of silence, allowing them to feel free, without embarrassment, to arrange themselves as they wish. If you're going off by yourself, you might want to think about whether a waterproof picnic rug, a camping chair or even a windbreak would be useful. A windbreak would not only offer shelter but also provide a bit of privacy if you are in a public setting.

Sitting for extended periods isn't good for anyone, and it's important to have the chance and freedom to move around. While it might seem obvious, the first step is to find a chair that is comfortable for you. We all come in different shapes and sizes, and so do chairs. If you need a cushion, find one or bring your own. Don't hesitate to switch seats if needed, especially since you'll be there most of the day. During tea and coffee breaks, if possible, it's beneficial to stand up and move around. Not only will it help with blood circulation but it will also aid in maintaining focus throughout the day. If you remain still for a long period, there's a tendency to nod off. If there is a garden or outdoor space, take the time to "smell the roses", to go and simply be out in creation, in the fresh air where you can breathe deeply.

For those who prefer to spend a day alone in reflection, intentionally walking any distance may not always be beneficial. I love nothing more than setting out for a long walk in the hills or beside a wooded river. Sometimes, when I am alone, those walks involve a prayerful conversation with God, either about what is on my mind or regarding what I observe as I walk; at other times, they do not. I simply walk and enjoy my surroundings. However, it is less easy to meditate on scripture unless it is intentionally part of your plan. If you are a walker who favours this option, I suggest taking a copy of one of the resources and beginning your day by sitting down to read through the first section. Reread the scripture several times before setting off. Then contemplate those things as you walk. Plan to stop again in about an hour and sit with the second section, repeating the process. Take a break for lunch and read the third section while you sit. Then reflect on it as you return to your starting point.

We have covered a great deal in this chapter, contemplating how God, as our Shepherd, guides us to peaceful and secure places amid life's chaotic hubbub. We've looked at our need to '"chew the cud" as we meditate on scripture and how we might hear God's voice. We've also gone over some practical steps we can take to avoid distraction. Remember, if we are truly to hear God's voice, we need to see and not just look, to listen and not just hear.

Questions to Ponder

Read Psalm 23 several times again. As you think back over the past six months, where have your green pastures and still waters been? Where are the places that restore you?

How often do you take time to "chew the cud", truly meditate on and extract everything you can from a verse of scripture? Do you need to actively choose to stop doing something else to rest in this way?

How have you heard God's voice in the past week? Was it visual or verbal? What did He say? Remember to be thankful for His presence with you.

Group Study

Which images from Psalm 23 truly spark your imagination? Share how you might encourage one another to find moments to "sit and chew the cud". What do you see as the difference between seeing and looking and between hearing versus simply listening?

Chapter 5

Where and When
to Find Quiet

"Yet the news about him spread all the more, so that crowds of people came to hear him and to be healed of their sicknesses. But Jesus often withdrew to lonely places and prayed" (Luke 5:15 – 16).

Throughout this book, I have often emphasised the importance of going away to spend time with God in silence, but why is this withdrawal from normal life necessary? We have already mentioned these verses from Psalm 139, reminding us that God's presence is everywhere: "Where can I go from your Spirit? Where can I flee from your presence?

If I go up to the heavens, you are there; if I make my bed in the depths, you are there.

If I rise on the wings of the dawn, if I settle on the far side of the sea, even there your hand will guide me, your right hand will hold me fast" (Psalms 139: 7 – 10).

If God is everywhere, why must I go somewhere else to find Him? It is not so much about locating God's presence elsewhere; it is more about our being more present in other places. Let me clarify what I mean: if I sit in my study, I am surrounded by photographs of friends and family, which often lead me on tangents from the task at hand. Perhaps I message them, or we end up having a chat on the phone. I have a pile of files, or worse, a heap of papers that I need to tend to, or my email notification beeps at me. No matter how hard I try, if I wish to be still and focus on God, I can be sure that these other tasks will resurface with an urgency they had never possessed before. So maybe I think I'll sit somewhere else in the house—well, that is futile, because suddenly that unfinished domestic chore that hasn't bothered me for days takes on an urgency that cannot be delayed any longer. Perhaps the weather is nice enough to sit out in the garden—fatal! I spot weeds that definitely weren't there yesterday, or I drift off into daydreams about what I could do with that flower bed or that bare patch of fence. You get the picture. Because this is where I live, work and spend my leisure time, this space is my domain, my place of responsibility, and it triggers many ongoing or unfinished tasks for me. If I am to be serious about giving God my full and undivided attention, then I must go somewhere else to at least minimise those distractions if not completely avoid them.

In the passage above from Luke 5, we learn that Jesus often withdrew to lonely places to pray. Mark 1:35 tells us, "Very early in the morning, while it was still dark, Jesus got up, left the house and went off to a solitary place, where he prayed." Meanwhile, Luke 6:12 states, "One of those days Jesus went out to a mountainside to pray, and spent the night praying to God." It was clearly a regular practice of Jesus to go away to be alone with His Father, to listen to Him (John 12:49), to seek His counsel (choosing the disciples Luke 6:12), as well as to intercede for others ("I have prayed for you..." Luke 22:32). While it could be argued that Jesus was escaping the crowds (Luke 5:15), He clearly developed a consistent habit of abandoning all distractions to seek God. He left the house where He was sleeping to find a quiet, solitary place, and yes, his bed was just as warm and comfortable as yours and mine!

Where might you go to find that special place outside of your everyday routine? While some may feel completely comfortable exploring that space, whether it's a park bench or sitting on a rock in the mountains, the unfortunate reality of society today is that many people feel quite vulnerable, especially when sitting alone in the countryside. Anxiety about the environment does not foster the freedom to wholeheartedly seek God.

Personally, another issue I have with park benches or coffee shops is that I am a self-confessed people-watcher. I love observing people and how they interact with each other; I also find myself wondering about those sitting alone and imagining all sorts of reasons in my mind. Therefore, being among others who are not gathered with the same purpose as me creates irresistible distractions. Perhaps you can tell that I am easily distracted?

For all these reasons, attending an organised Quiet Day, where there is space to sit alone with minimal distractions yet the comfort of being in discreet company with others engaged in the same activity, seems like a very beneficial option. For extroverts, there is the added appeal of being able to interact during breaks with those on the same journey. I would love to say that all you need to do is Google "Quiet Days" in your area and you will find several options to choose from. Sadly, that is rarely the case. If you know of a Christian retreat centre or a centre for Christian spirituality near you, it would be worth checking their programmes. Numerous dioceses within the Church of England have a spirituality network (or similar) and may be able to connect you with organised Quiet Days. Other denominations may have similar facilities. There is a handy little booklet produced annually by the Retreats Association called 'Retreats', which lists over 150 retreat centres across the UK and beyond. Although not all of them may offer organised Quiet Days, they may have spaces that you can book to enjoy time away by yourself. Many of these places may also offer a residential programme with the possibility of attending a retreat for several days, which may or may not be in total silence. Some may be led or guided, while others may simply provide a safe space for you to find your own quiet time.

One person I know admits that for them, a single day is not enough, as they find that taking several days helps them to switch off and then deliberately focus their attention on God.

When I lived in the southeast of England, there were several centres nearby as well as a couple of churches that regularly held a programme of Quiet Days, so it was not difficult to find something suitable.

However, having recently moved to a different part of the country, I thought I would book myself onto a Quiet Day for Lent. Despite my best efforts, I only managed to find one, and that was on a day when I was unavailable. Therefore, I completely understand if you have difficulty finding one. For that reason alone, it's easy to shrug our shoulders and say, "Well, I tried...," and leave it there, causing any resolve we may have had to ebb away in disappointment.

The pandemic and subsequent lockdown gave many of us the time (if not the space) to be still, ponder, reflect and pray. As a result, many continue to seek out those moments of stillness. A growing desire for quiet spirituality has led to increased interest in Quiet Days; however, opportunities have not kept pace with this interest. While it may seem like a significant step to move from seeking a quiet space for oneself to facilitating a day for others, the following chapter offers practical advice on how to host and run a Quiet Day. Resources in the final section can easily serve as material for the day.

As a footnote to this section, I recognise that, for very valid reasons, it may not always be possible for someone to leave their own home, and I would like to consider an alternative way of being separate. This might also be beneficial for those who simply wish to create a meaningful space for their daily quiet time within a busy household.

Some people find it helpful to have a specific chair or space in the house where they sit or kneel to pray. That place is reserved solely for that purpose and is not typically used at other times. For many years, I have had a comfortable chair in my study for that purpose. When I am at my desk, I am usually there to work, but if I sit in the other chair, well, that's my prayer chair. Visiting that place is an act of stepping away from the normal routine. I remember visiting a friend who had transformed a broom cupboard into a tiny chapel in his house, complete with a simple cross, a candle and a prayer stool. Someone else sits at a designated spot at their dining table and lights a candle, which signifies that special space for them. People can be very inventive.

The story is told of Susanna Wesley, famously the mother of John and Charles, although she actually gave birth to a total of nineteen children, including two sets of twins! Even amid the most complex and busy years of her life as a mother, she still scheduled two hours each day for fellowship with God and time in His Word, and she adhered to that schedule faithfully. The challenge was finding a place of privacy in a house filled to overflowing with children.

Mother Wesley's solution was to bring her Bible to her favourite chair and drape her long apron over her head, creating a kind of tent. This resembled the "tent of meeting", the tabernacle from the days of Moses in the Old Testament. Everyone in the household, from the smallest toddler to the oldest domestic helpers, understood to respect this sign. When Susanna was under the apron, she was with God and was not to be disturbed except in the case of the most serious emergency. In the privacy of her little tent, she interceded for her husband and children and delved into the deep mysteries of God in the scriptures. This holy discipline gave her a thorough and profound knowledge of the Bible. I'm certainly not suggesting we follow her exact example; we live in very different times, but we can be inventive in finding the time and space available to us. It's hard to imagine how this was even possible for Mrs Wesley, but perhaps it encourages us to be just a little more disciplined in our efforts to set aside quiet times for God.

Many retreat centres now offer online content, sharing organised Quiet Day material via Zoom, which is an excellent option for those unable to leave their own homes. Once again, more details about these can be found in the pamphlet 'Retreats' or through a Google search.

We have considered Quiet Days, which are probably no more than four or five hours, and short residential retreats. I would like to briefly explore the other end of the spectrum and how longer periods of reflection might potentially fit into the wider rhythm of our lives.

You will recall that before He began His three years of intensive, itinerant ministry, Jesus spent 40 days and nights in the wilderness, praying and fasting, which clearly formed the preparation He needed for what was to come. To the best of our knowledge, this was a unique, lifetime experience. (See also Resource 4.)

None of us will ever undertake what Jesus did, but throughout history, there are many examples of saints engaging in lengthy periods of prayer and seclusion. The Desert Fathers are perhaps the most notable, but there have been many others as well. What about us? Is it possible to incorporate this into the modern world?

I know a couple who, between each major job change, take one to three months for what they call a sabbatical. Essentially, it is a time for them to reflect on their previous ministry, allowing themselves to process the good, the bad and the ugly of that period before looking forward to what is to come. This does not mean they have spent three months on their knees, hidden away, immersed in their Bibles. Instead, it has been a time of holiday and rest as well as an opportunity to reflect with God, each other and potentially friends, on all that has transpired and what might lie ahead. I recognise that not everyone may have the luxury of such times, but a deliberate, intentional break from our normal lives can be immensely valuable.

Somewhere between those extremes, there must be a balanced and achievable possibility for each of us, one that is longer than a daily quiet time but shorter than a 40-day fast or a two-month sabbatical. Where might you find a window of time?

We are told in Luke 5 that Jesus regularly withdrew. What counts as regular may differ between individuals, but I know this: unless it is scheduled in the diary and regarded as a priority, that dedicated time will not happen, and certainly not regularly. We see from the passages examined earlier in this chapter that Jesus took time, or perhaps made time, early in the morning, and there were occasions when he prayed all night. Depending on one's stage of life and/or work schedule, giving up sleep may seem impossible. However, that does not mean we shouldn't consider it a possibility. For a young mother with broken nights and full days, or a business executive juggling family life and international travel, we can sympathise; yet, all of us make time for the things that are important to us. Many would testify that sacrificing sleep to pray has yielded some of the most precious and personal encounters with God. Moreover, far from feeling tired and exhausted, they have felt energised and empowered for the day ahead. I remember a wedding guest who attended an all-night prayer meeting at their church, only getting to bed at 7 am for a couple of hours' sleep before the wedding yet was bright and full of life throughout the whole day and evening. I believe that when we make sacrificial choices for God, He honours us in ways we might not imagine.

I recently heard someone say, "There's no such thing as not enough time, just the wrong priorities." When considering priorities, you may have come across a helpful visual aid: a pile of rocks, a pile of gravel, a pile of sand and a jug of water all placed next to a large bucket. If the water, sand and gravel are added first, there will be no room for the rocks without the water overflowing and the rocks protruding from the top. However, if you place the rocks first, then add the gravel, followed by the sand and then the water, there will be space for all the components. If you haven't seen it, try it yourself. It's a great sermon illustration. The lesson is, of course, that if you prioritise the big things—i.e., schedule the priorities first—then add in the important, less important and so on, there is enough time for everything; and even if there isn't, hopefully, it will be the inconsequential things that get dropped.

In his excellent book 'Practising the Way', John Mark Comer, speaking about spiritual formation, says, "'I'm too busy' is the number one excuse/obstacle to formation. The hard truth is, most of us waste copious amounts of time. Cue all the stats: the average millennial is on their phone nearly four hours a day; most adults aged 35 to 44 watch two to three hours of TV a day. Combined, that's almost a full-time job. Think what we could do with even a tithe of that time." Spiritual formation and "time out with God" are, inevitably, closely linked.

How significant is your spiritual health and well-being to you? How can you make time to tend to your spiritual healthcare? The bonus is that doing so might also benefit more than just your spiritual health. Your mental and physical health could also benefit from the break.

In the days when I used to drive out into the countryside for a day of reviewing and reflecting, it was also the era of physical paper diaries—well, a Filofax, actually. I would simply put a line through the entire day and absolutely prioritise it. I defended it fiercely. Nowadays, you can block out the day electronically so that neither you nor anyone else can schedule an appointment on that day. None of us, regardless of how important we believe our roles to be, are indispensable 24/7. Even Jesus. While it may be difficult for us to understand walking away from someone desperately seeking our help, that is exactly what Jesus did repeatedly. We read in Luke 5:15–16 that, "Yet the news about him spread all the more, so that crowds of people came to hear him and to be healed of their sicknesses. But Jesus often withdrew to lonely places and prayed." Contrary to what we might imagine or believe as we read the Gospels, Jesus did not heal everyone who was sick. We need not look far for proof. We only need to think of the crippled man begging outside the temple, mentioned in Acts 3, whom Peter and John encountered as they went to pray. We are told that he was crippled from birth and was brought there every day to beg. Jesus must have passed by him too, but He had not been moved by the Spirit to heal the man. Similarly, at the Pool of Bethesda mentioned in John 5, when Jesus healed the paralysed man, we are told that many sick and disabled gathered there; clearly, Jesus did not heal them all or we would have heard about it. Only that one man was healed by Jesus that day.

Jesus trusted that the Holy Spirit within Him would guide Him on what to do, whom to speak to and whom to heal, and He relied on God's care for everyone else. Sometimes we are misled into thinking everything depends solely on us. Others may place many demands on our time, often unnecessarily or unfairly, making us believe we are the only solution to their needs. If I walk away or take a day's annual leave, will the consequences really be so severe? Of course, we should be aware of others' needs but not at the cost of our own well-being. Honestly, if our lives become too stressful, taking time out can be the best choice, not just for us but also for those around us, especially if it helps us return calmer and with a clearer sense of purpose. Time alone with God is not wasted; it is essential.

Unless you now have the freedom to book a regular day, rather than diving in headfirst and feeling the need to set aside a whole day each week or month, start by doing something realistic like booking a Quiet Day in Lent or Advent, which is when many places specifically organise Quiet Days to prepare for the biggest Christian festivals. Once you have attended one or two, you may feel encouraged to do more. Different rhythms work for different people, but please don't be misled into thinking that once this project is finished, or once the children have left home, or once you are retired, then you will have time. Believe me, I've experienced all those scenarios, and time never magically becomes available; it always requires an intentional and deliberate effort on our part to create that time. The choice is ours.

Another ideal time to consider a Quiet Day or even a longer retreat is when you face a decision or need to reflect on a significant life question. We all make hundreds of decisions each day, from what time we wake up and what we wear to the moment we fall back into bed; life requires us to make decisions. Therefore, we decide throughout our day. Some choices are made instantly (tea or coffee?) while others may take weeks or even months. If we lived in perfect harmony with God as Jesus did, much of that decision-making would happen naturally, guiding us to make wise and accurate choices; unfortunately, this is not the case for most of us. However, when it comes to making major, life-changing decisions, why wouldn't we consciously set aside undisturbed time to seek God's counsel?

We read that before choosing His disciples—those who would be with Him and lead the early, emerging church—Jesus spent the entire night in prayer (Luke 6:12 – 16). However, I am certain that was not the only time He prayed and sought His Father on this matter; perhaps that was the night of the final shortlisting. Even for Jesus, seeking God's guidance was a necessary and vital part of His life. And then there were those last agonising, gut-wrenching hours of prayer hidden away in the Garden of Gethsemane (Matthew 26:36 – 44), when Jesus moved apart even from His closest disciples, which marked the final hours of earnest preparation for what was to come as His last days unfolded before His glorious resurrection.

Taking time out of a busy schedule can feel overwhelming, but let me encourage you. The ministry that my husband and I were involved in at Ashburnham Place in Sussex was partly aimed at encouraging the entire community, who lived and/or worked on site, to engage in ongoing, gathered prayer. This required having at least two, but preferably more, people in the prayer room for each hour. We decided, with the full agreement of the trustees, to tithe the working time of every member of staff. This had significant consequences for us, ensuring that all our guest care, as well as other responsibilities, were managed properly. It was truly fascinating to observe how often those who paused to fulfil their prayer commitment completed their work more effectively and efficiently than those who chose not to undertake their allocated hours, as they already felt pressured by their workload. When individuals took a bold step of faith, uncertain about how their work would be accomplished, they often testified that they needn't have worried about it!

Questions to Ponder

Read through Psalms 42:1 – 6 several times. What questions do these verses raise for you? How will you respond?

Consider where and how you might detach yourself from the realities of your daily routines. What locations and activities might suit you?

If you haven't already, look into the options available locally and ask for recommendations for a Quiet Day.

If going on your own feels too big a step, whom might you ask to accompany you?

Group Study

There may be many things that terrify you, but share what inspires you about Susannah Wesley's life. How easy or difficult do you find it to make time for your spiritual well-being, especially when other demands are upon you? Encourage those who feel too overwhelmed to prioritise their own well-being and relationship with God. In what ways could your group support them?

Chapter 6
Planning A Quiet Day
A Practical Guide

This chapter provides a practical guide for those thinking about hosting a Quiet Day themselves. Before dismissing it as irrelevant to you, consider whether you might gather two or three like-minded friends and organise a day together. Nothing elaborate is necessary—just an informal gathering, possibly using the resources in this book or creating your own materials. Regardless of your thoughts, there may be some tips here to help you on your journey. However, I am primarily approaching this from the perspective of organising something for a group, whether it be a home group or another church-based group, extending the offer to the wider church community or even beyond. As mentioned earlier, there is a shortage of organised Quiet Days in certain areas, so arranging one yourself might be your best option.

Who Will Run the Event?

First, consider partnering with someone. The majority of the time, Jesus sent his disciples out in twos to undertake even the most mundane tasks, and there is great wisdom in following that principle. Not only does it share the load, but it also allows each of you to play to your strengths. You will both have different perspectives and notice various aspects that may require attention. I recall that when we were at Ashburnham, we had a fantastic lady on the team who was brilliant at hosting our house parties and other events. She had a genuine gift for connecting with people and engaging them in conversation, even those who could be quite challenging and required extra patience. I was in awe of her; personally, I found hosting house parties exhausting and often looked for an escape route. Conversely, I was very comfortable being upfront, welcoming guests to meetings, giving notices and, at times, speaking at events. It didn't faze me at all. On one occasion, our speaker cancelled at very short notice, and I had to step in. Not wanting the guests to listen to me for the entire day, I asked my wonderful colleague if she would just do the welcome and the notices, which, to my mind, was not a difficult task. She looked utterly horrified and explained that she couldn't possibly stand in front of everyone and speak. It was a moment of absolute clarity for me when I realised that what one finds easy and natural is utterly terrifying for another and vice versa.

Having two people also means that one can focus on welcoming guests into the space while the other can busy themselves checking that the kettle is switched on and organising the drinks. In contrast, if you try to run the whole thing alone, you may end up feeling pulled in different directions and giving off an air of anything but peace, which would be completely self-defeating. Partnering with one or two others adds an element of accountability for both yourself and those who attend. Broader accountability should also be considered, and it may be wise to discuss your plans with your minister or pastor before proceeding. They might have additional ideas, experience or contacts and may wish to be involved. It is only courteous to ensure they are fully informed of your intentions. They will also be able to advise on any safeguarding issues you may need to consider.

Who Will Come, and the Merits of Advertising and Booking

If you're unsure of your ability and want to build confidence, don't hesitate to start small. Three or four people might be enough to begin with. You can always invite more as your confidence increases. Have you discussed spending intentional time alone with God in your home group or church? Are you aware of others who have shown interest in having a Quiet Day? Begin by approaching them and forming a small group through word of mouth. Perhaps you're in a small group that has been reading this book together; start right there.

If you already feel confident about advertising it more widely, consider how many people you would be comfortable having in your chosen venue (we'll discuss venues shortly). What is the maximum number of people you could comfortably gather in one place while ensuring there is enough space for participants to sit individually without disturbing one another?

If you intend to advertise the day, consider the wording carefully. In addition to the essential information of where and when (date plus start and end times), it's crucial to think about what people will actually read and the assumptions they may make. For instance, if you advertise a Quiet Day, what does that actually mean for most people? A day of sitting in silence trying to be "holy"? Be as descriptive as possible using simple, non-jargon words while also keeping it as brief as you can; the reality is that most people don't read lengthy notices. Furthermore, a "day" might sound quite a daunting length of time. Perhaps consider something like "This will be an opportunity to explore the story of (Mary and Martha) through input from (x) followed by short times of quiet personal reflection."

Also, consider the visual impact of any advertising. An image is very helpful in attracting interest, but what does the picture communicate, and to whom might it appeal? While I must be careful not to over-generalise, if you want to encourage men, for example, a pair of muddy walking boots and a rucksack may be more likely to catch their attention than a vase of flowers.

Remember to include practical details, such as whether lunch will be provided or if participants need to bring their own packed lunch. Also clarify if there is a cost, a suggested donation or if it is free. Make it clear how they should book and consider what details you need from participants. Once people have booked, I usually send a follow-up email providing more information about the day such as where to park or any helpful travel instructions, a detailed outline of the day's schedule, including timings for coffee, tea and lunch breaks, as well as what items they might find useful to bring along. For instance, a Bible, a notebook or journal, plus crayons, paints and a sketch pad, if that helps them. If you plan to use outdoor space, suggest suitable clothing and footwear. If you are using a home and have a shoes-off-at-the-door policy, invite them to bring slippers if they wish. Let them know what you will be providing, including hot drinks, and if you are providing food, remember to check for any special dietary requirements.

Don't be afraid to keep a waiting list if you are oversubscribed. Set your boundaries and stick to them. It's much better for those who arrive to feel relaxed and at ease than for everyone to feel crowded and uncomfortable.

Venues

There are several options to consider, each with its own advantages and disadvantages; however, you will need to decide what works best for you and those who might attend.

Someone's home: As a clergy spouse, I have had the privilege of living in some quite large houses, and many of the Quiet Days I have hosted have been in my own home. However, I recognise that this is not practical or feasible for many people. Do you know someone else with a sufficiently large home? Usually, my living room can seat up to twelve people, which has always been my maximum (including myself). It is not reasonable to expect someone to sit on the floor or perch on a stool, so how many could you seat?

In addition to the gathered space, ensure there are also twelve individual spaces available for people to use, although not necessarily twelve separate rooms; that would be quite a large house! Arrange the rooms so that two or three people can be alone and unhindered. In my experience, several people will always remain in the main meeting room rather than move to another area. I have also been fortunate enough to have garden space, and if the weather is suitable, I arrange chairs strategically around the garden for people to use.

Once the children had left home, I would also use the guest bedrooms, usually guiding trusted friends to make use of those spaces. This option is unavailable if you have children or vulnerable family members living at home, nor would it be fair to intrude upon their home in this manner.

For and against? It is convenient, and there is no cost involved; many people enjoy the feeling of being welcomed into a home. It can require a lot of preparation—tidying up and cleaning—especially if, like me, housework only gets done when absolutely necessary! A certain level of tidiness is necessary, as people may find excessive clutter and personal belongings distracting or even unsettling.

A church or church hall can be a good option, but it also has some drawbacks. There is something special about being in a place of worship, with all the focus and imagery making you feel close to God. You should consider where is best to gather everyone and create a focal point that is sufficiently intimate without making people feel huddled in a corner or seated in rows of pews. Will there be enough comfortable seating and perhaps somewhere for people to sit and write or draw? Will it be warm enough? When people sit for a while, their body temperature drops, making them feel the cold more keenly. Is there a risk of others, such as cleaners or flower arrangers entering the building to attend to their duties, potentially causing a disturbance or distraction? Might other groups be using nearby rooms? For instance, you wouldn't want to compete with a toddler group. Are members of the church leadership team attending the day? If so, for them, this may be their workplace, and those urgent, pressing jobs could draw their attention away, or the church warden might sit and list all the things needing attention instead of taking time aside.

This may also be a no-cost option; however, that cannot be assumed. Always check availability and expectations.

Retreat centres could be a great option, especially since they are staffed and designed specifically for this purpose. There will be spaces both to gather and to disperse, but they will come at a cost. Consider what people might be willing to pay and whether they would be willing to travel. Will some need to leave early to pick up children from school, etc.?

Costs

Be realistic about the costs of organising the day. Besides the venue and refreshments, consider the implications of inviting someone else to lead the event. It is only fair to cover their travel expenses and think about the time they have spent preparing, as well as the time they spend with you on the day itself. Money can be an awkward topic to discuss, but it's best to address these matters before booking. Some people may not expect payment, but that does not mean you should not offer it.

I remember trying to book a well-known speaker for an event at Ashburnham. Before I could discuss the honorarium we would offer (which was very generous), she somewhat forcefully told me her daily rate, which was actually lower than our proposed honorarium. It felt as though she assumed we wanted her for nothing. Needless to say, I didn't engage her. However, there is another side to that; I also remember leading a two-day retreat for an organised group, for which I had spent several days preparing as well as travelling some distance. In addition to the two days of the retreat, I received a scented candle and a bunch of flowers. While those gifts are nice to receive, I believe it is important to genuinely value the contributions that people make, and this should be factored into the event costs.

When I have hosted Quiet Days in my own home, I ask for a contribution to cover the food costs without specifying an exact amount. I clarify that any excess money will be donated to a specific charity. I leave information leaflets about the charity for people to pick up if they wish, placed beside a basket for participants' donations. I never check to ensure everyone has contributed, allowing them the freedom to decide how much to give. Providing people with a choice is helpful. There may be those who, for very good reasons, cannot contribute, and no one should feel discouraged from attending such a day. I have always covered my food costs comfortably and have been able to send a generous gift as well.

Creating a Peaceful Atmosphere

Whichever venue you select, there are certain aspects you will want to ensure to create a welcoming, comfortable atmosphere where people can engage as fully as possible with the day's purpose.

We have already considered the intrusion of noise from other venue users, but we should also think about whether anything else might unnecessarily disturb the atmosphere. For example, if you are offering a meal, make sure all potentially noisy elements are prepared in advance so that you do not have to switch on an electric whisk or food processor, especially if your kitchen is close to where people will be seated quietly.

Sometimes things are beyond our control. Once, we gathered at a house surrounded by a large garden with a sizeable pond. It was a lovely summer's day, so we decided to spend the entire day outside instead of indoors. As we gathered on the patio beside the pond, the neighbour who hired contract gardeners chose that day to have all their hedges trimmed. The noise of power cutters and leaf blowers echoed around us, amplified by the water. Not to be outdone, the neighbour on the other side took that opportunity to demolish their rather large and derelict greenhouse, so during a lull in the power tools, the sounds of smashing glass and timber being tossed into a skip became quite noticeable. In a distant field, a tractor laboured through the heavy clay soil. And then, to top it all off, as we sat enjoying our lunch, the Red Arrows flew overhead! I have never seen them there before or since, but they chose our Quiet Day to make an appearance. All we could do was laugh. Hopefully, that won't be your experience, but we must trust that God can use even what may seem to us a disaster, for His greater purposes.

Assuming you plan to meet indoors, consider the temperature as the day goes on. If possible, increase the thermostat a few degrees to maintain a comfortable environment while attendees remain inactive. However, avoid making the room too stuffy, as this may cause people to inadvertently nod off.

Conversely, if you are meeting in a room with large glass windows, ensure there are adequate blinds or shading to prevent overheating from sunlight or being blinded by glare.

Think about where people will sit during moments of silence. How can you make them more comfortable? If they will sit on pews, consider offering cushions, a rug or a blanket. If the gathering is at a home, ensure the space is clean, tidy and free of excessive clutter from personal belongings. Aim for a neutral atmosphere.

Some attendees of Quiet Days have observed that having a desk, table or other solid surface for writing is very helpful. Additionally, it is important to ensure there is sufficient lighting. If there are table lamps or other lights, turn them all on before attendees arrive to avoid anyone having to search for switches or feeling too embarrassed to find them.

Discreet boxes of tissues placed around the area are a considerate touch. Tears often flow when God is touching hearts, and there's nothing worse than becoming snotty without being able to find a tissue!

When welcoming guests, ensure they know where the toilets are and highlight all options for personal reflection. Additionally, if relevant, point out areas they should avoid. Be clear about when the period of silence will end, how you will communicate this and where to reconvene afterwards, whether in your main meeting space or elsewhere for coffee, etc. I always enjoyed using my grandmother's dinner gong, which produced a beautiful, soft reverberating sound that was both loud and gentle at the same time.

Consider the needs of those who are neurodivergent, as they may find it extremely difficult to sit still. Having a fidget spinner, some playdough or even some knitting may help them relax enough to focus on what is being said and could also assist them during times of silence.

Ensure you do everything possible to create a safe and peaceful environment that alleviates any fears or anxieties people may have. Thoughtfully considering small and simple actions in advance can help stressed individuals to relax, especially if they are already feeling apprehensive or uncertain about what to expect.

Offering Hospitality and/or Keeping Silence

There is quite a debate about whether participants should stay silent all day or if offering hospitality creates a chance for conversation. Honestly, everyone will have their own preferences, and I think it's best to offer what you personally feel most comfortable with.

Consider what you can realistically provide and why you are doing so. For example, if you can only offer water and hot drinks, encourage attendees to bring their own packed lunch. This way, participants can choose to eat together as a group or enjoy the freedom to eat alone in silence. Alternatively, you might serve a simple meal of bread and soup, which requires minimal preparation on the day, provided the soup is already prepared. This creates a gathering point and can be enjoyed in silence or not, according to preference.

As you may already have realised, I love to be hospitable. For me, sharing my home as a place to meet with God also involves trying to bless those who come with generous hospitality. Unless you are Superman or Superwoman, this definitely needs to be done with someone else. It's simply not possible to welcome, lead and serve a lovely meal, along with all the cooking and clearing up, on your own. While you can prepare as much as possible beforehand, there will inevitably be things that need doing at the last minute. Providing a meal means this will definitely not be a quiet day for you. You may be facilitating it for others, but there will be little chance for you or your helpers to be still and quiet. If others are assisting, make sure they are fully committed to the day's vision; otherwise, they might not be as alert to the need for peace and quiet.

I have used the term "generous hospitality", by which I mean considering things that will be special to people; don't buy the cheapest biscuits if you can afford better. Get something special. Similarly, I often bake a couple of cakes for teatime, although these are also available at all good supermarkets. I usually prefer to prepare something relatively simple for lunch rather than something with multiple components. Perhaps lasagne with a side salad and garlic bread or cottage pie. Another straightforward option is a cold lunch with sliced meats and pre-prepared salads. I generally provide a simple dessert too, though a fruit bowl may suffice. People do not necessarily want an enormous lunch, and again, there is the risk of people falling asleep if they are overfed.

Another aspect of generous hospitality is being friendly and open, putting people at ease. Sharing lunch together fosters warmth and conversation, which may or may not centre around what has happened in the morning sessions. However, for some individuals, such social interaction might feel intrusive on a day they've dedicated to God. This may be especially true for a group that does not know each other well. If this is the case, the packed lunch option will give individuals a choice.

Whatever you decide to do, start small and simple, and grow your offering only when you feel ready or able.

Creating a Focal Point

We will examine the specific content for the day in the next chapter, but depending on your level of creativity, you might want to create a focal point for the day in the main gathering space. At its simplest, this could be just a cross, a lit candle or an open Bible. For those feeling more imaginative, there are many possibilities for using various materials. Different pieces of coloured fabric in a range of textures can be very helpful. For example, you could place a large pot or jug on its side with a piece of blue cloth flowing out of it to symbolise water. Some resources include ideas for a creative focal point, although the options are unlimited.

It might be helpful for individuals to take something from that display to hold or look at during their time alone. For example, you could add blue or clear glass floristry beads to the "water", which would also enhance the texture of the water effect.

A focal point can also be used at the end of the day as a form of worship or to express what God has been communicating to them. For instance, you might invite people to write something on a Post-it note, which they then fold and place on the cross, or to add a stone into the water, symbolising something they wish to entrust to God's eternal love and mercy.

All of this is completely optional. The important thing is that people come to listen to God, not to admire your creative talent, so remember to keep the main thing the main thing.

Ending the Day

Ultimately, this will rely on you, your group and what you deem comfortable. Options to consider include the following:

You could choose not to reconvene after the last section of silence and let people drift away when they are ready. This might feel somewhat untidy, and you may need to check that everyone has left, which could be a bit awkward—especially if you find someone deep in prayer an hour later while you're waiting to lock up. This situation could be avoided by finishing with a cup of tea at a set time.

A simple way to foster a more collective feeling is to gather everyone in the main meeting space and suggest they sit quietly and pray silently, offering to God all they have experienced that day and all they are heading towards. Personally, I would not suggest that they pray for each other during the silence as, although they have been on this journey together, it has likely been a very personal encounter for each individual. As the leader, you could conclude this time of prayer after a few minutes by simply saying "Amen" to signify the end.

Depending on your tradition, you may want to write a short prayer or even create a brief act of worship with a liturgy and responses appropriate for the passage you have been engaging with. This could include an interactive exercise as suggested above. Alternatively, you might provide copies of a Compline (Night Prayer) service to share together; however, with all these options, care must be taken not to disrupt what God may be doing, requiring sensitivity to the Spirit's guidance.

Another option might be to listen to a piece of music or a worship song, but this should be approached with sensitivity.

To Share or not to Share?

You are the best person to gauge the group dynamics and determine what seems appropriate. In any group, there will be those eager to share what God has been saying to them alongside those who would prefer not to attend if they feel required to speak to the group. It is important to recognise the needs of both and to ensure everyone feels comfortable and heard. Unless I am leading a group of people who are well acquainted and familiar with each other's quirks, I would refrain from inviting a group to share how their day has been. I feel that God may have touched on some deeply personal issues, which are their business alone, not mine. In such cases, I might ask them over tea afterwards how they have found the day. That way, people can share if they wish to, but there is no obligation to do so. Additionally, individuals may feel safer speaking with one or two others rather than the entire group. Moreover, if someone is domineering or insensitive to the needs of others, they can still feel heard without dominating the whole group.

To Pray or not to Pray?

Don't get me wrong, I'm not questioning whether you should pray! Hopefully, you and your co-worker(s) have been prayerfully preparing every aspect of the day and praying for those who will attend. I would also pray for the group after the opening welcome and often offer a time of silence for people to lay down whatever they have come with and entrust to God those for whom they feel a particular burden.

What I am discussing here is whether to offer to pray with or for people individually throughout the day. My personal view is that this is not what people have come for, and it is not what I am offering. First and foremost, people have come to spend personal time with God in a safe environment; they have not come for prayer ministry or to hear what someone else may say or pray for them (even if that is what they desire). This may seem a little harsh, especially to those who are more pastorally minded, but I believe it is essential to make the distinction between what is being offered, which is primarily about creating and facilitating a space to be alone with God. However, I am not entirely lacking in compassion, and if someone appears visibly distressed, I would offer to pray with them briefly, possibly direct them to an appropriate verse of scripture to reflect on and send them back to their own place with God.

A longer retreat is entirely different, and I would approach it in a markedly different way.

Timings/Programme

I recognise that I have written extensively about "days". If you are just starting out, you might want to consider focusing on just a morning, so I have also included a suggested timetable for that. Firstly, a note of caution: whatever time you plan to start the programme, bring it forward by at least fifteen minutes because there will always be those who arrive at the last possible moment. Often, this is for genuine reasons, but latecomers can be very disruptive if you are trying to create a peaceful atmosphere.

The start and end times are sufficient for general advertising of the day. You could send out a programme to those who book or simply have it available on the day so that people know where they are meant to be and when.

When organising the timetable, also think about those attending. Are they parents who need to drop off and collect children from school? How will the timings suit them, or will people be free to stay longer? Which day of the week will you select? A Saturday means that those who work during the week are more likely to attend, but it is often a busy family day and might exclude some. If you are planning a series of Quiet Days, choose a memorable day, such as the first Friday or third Thursday of the month, as a helpful reminder.

Suggested timings might look like this:

Quiet Morning

9:45 am   Arrival (this will be your advertised
               time to start)

10:00 am   Welcome & first input

10:15 am	Quiet
11:00 am	Coffee break
11:15 am	Second input
11:30 am	Quiet
12:15 pm	Final gathering
12:30 pm	Depart

Alternatively, you could begin with cakes and pastries at 9:45 am and remove the coffee break in order to end by 12:15 pm.

Quiet Day

9:45 am	Arrival (this will be your advertised time to start)
10:00 am	Welcome & first input
10:15 am	Quiet
11:15 am	Coffee break
11:30 am	Second input
11:30 am	Quiet
12:30 pm	Lunch (if you are serving lunch, it will take everyone a little while to get to the loo, so plan to serve it about 12:40

even though the programme will say 12:30)

1:30 pm   Third input

1:45 pm   Quiet

2:45 pm   Final gathering

3:00 pm   Tea (this gives people the option to slip away if they need to)

You could consider adding another session in the afternoon if you wish, but for most people, three sessions tend to work well.

MARGARET WOODING JONES

Chapter 7

Introduction to Resources

Most of the resources that follow are organised into three sessions, each ending with ideas to use in the quiet space, including questions to ask or thoughts to pursue. The guidance notes for each session of silence are provided merely to spark ideas and are not obligatory, but they may be helpful if you feel a bit stuck. You might only have time to focus fully on one of the ideas. No matter; they serve as guides or pointers.

For those who purely want some brief guidance on using a passage of scripture alone, you may prefer simply to use the Quiet Reflections and not read through the lesson notes at all. This may give sufficient structure, especially if your time is more limited, although do allow yourself sufficient time for honest reflection. God may have a completely different plan for you, so remain open to the Spirit. Follow Him, not me!

If using this material in a group rather than individually, the leader can simply read the session notes aloud. However, it will sound more authentic if you personalise them by adding your own illustrations or life experiences instead of mine.

If you wish to use the Quiet Reflection resources for an organised Quiet Day, print the guidance notes for each section on small slips of paper for participants to take with them. However, do not print all three sections together and distribute them at once. The day naturally progresses, with each session building on the previous one, so it's best to provide only what is needed for that specific period of quiet. No matter how much you ask attendees not to read the other sections, they will inevitably do so. This may create a sense of being overwhelmed by choice or of missing out on something that could have been an important step along the way.

Each of the resources contains one key scripture, sometimes just a verse or two, sometimes a parable or event, but always the passage is relatively brief. This is deliberate to help maintain focus and potentially aid in recalling the passage later. I remember when I attended my first entirely silent retreat in Oxfordshire; the nun leading it asked whether I would be comfortable with just one verse to focus on for the next three days. To be honest, I was a little anxious, but I agreed to try. That was fine until she told me what the verse was! The fact that I can still recall it over 30 years later shows it must have had a significant impact on me, but the verse was John 1:38, which says, "Turning around, Jesus saw them following and asked, 'What do you want?' They said, 'Rabbi' (which means 'Teacher'), 'where are you staying?'" It is truly extraordinary what can be gleaned from a single verse if you are willing to sit with it. If you use the resources consistently, you will notice a pattern emerging in most, but not all, of the chapters. The first section of the day deliberately concentrates on God, allowing participants to look up and beyond their own concerns or questions. It goes without saying that as we meditate on God's greatness, our own lives are put more fully into perspective.

Consider the words of Psalms 121:1 – 4, which speak so eloquently of this shift in perspective: "I lift up my eyes to the mountains—where does my help come from? My help comes from the Lord, the Maker of heaven and earth … indeed, he who watches over Israel will neither slumber nor sleep."

As the psalmist gazes at the mighty mountains surrounding him, seeking inspiration and strength, he is reminded that God is not only bigger and stronger than the mountains but that He is their very Maker. His heart is lifted in worship, and his focus shifts away from himself and his responsibilities as a leader in Israel, firmly resting on God. That is our desire as we prepare to listen to Him.

As you start your time of quiet with God, there's no better focus for your eyes (and ears) than on Him, allowing yourself to look and listen to Him while letting all other thoughts fade away.

The second section usually begins to focus on how this particular scripture can influence our own lives. We are reminded in Proverbs 4:23, "Above all else, guard your heart, for everything you do flows from it." Therefore, this section mainly concerns how you might establish those guards—a time for a little spiritual check-up. Verses 24 – 26 continue, "Keep your mouth free of perversity; keep corrupt talk far from your lips. Let your eyes look straight ahead, fix your gaze directly before you. Give careful thought to the paths for your feet and be steadfast in all your ways." Or as the writer to the Hebrews expressed it, "Let us throw off everything that hinders and the sin that so easily entangles. And let us run with perseverance the race marked out for us, fixing our eyes on Jesus, the pioneer and perfecter of faith" (Hebrews 12:1 – 2). If the first section was about worship and wonder, then this part concerns self-examination. We do so safely in the light of and with the aid of the One we worship. We are opening ourselves up to His touch and His voice; there is no room here for self-condemnation or judgement. This is about partnering with what He is revealing to us.

The final section of the day usually focuses on reflecting on what we will put into practice, what needs to change or what we might implement as a result of engaging with this scripture. We are reminded of the importance of translating our spiritual learning into practical action by the Apostle James in his Epistle. He clearly states, "What good is it, my brothers and sisters, if someone claims to have faith but has no deeds? Can such faith save them? Suppose a brother or sister is without clothes and daily food. If one of you says to them, 'Go in peace; keep warm and well fed,' but does nothing about their physical needs, what good is it? In the same way, faith by itself, if it is not accompanied by action, is dead" (James 2:14 – 17). One might almost say that James was being very blunt and direct, but here lies the truth. We all live in a broken, messy and hurting world, and we are daily faced with that reality, whether it is in our personal relationships, as we go about our daily routines or as we listen to the relentless media storm of bad news. While it can be wonderful, and I would argue essential, to take time aside to be quiet and still, that is not a place where we can remain permanently, no matter how much we might wish to. As our relationship with God grows, develops and matures, we may learn to carry that quietness and stillness with us even as we engage with the brokenness around us.

Do you remember Isaiah worshipping in the temple and having a vision of God's glory filling the space? (Isaiah 6). As he gazes at this wondrous vision of God, he is suddenly convicted of his own sin, which is quickly dealt with by a burning coal placed on his lips. But do you remember what happened next? God sent him out with a message, and as a result, we have, among other things, some of the clearest prophetic scriptures pointing the way towards the coming Messiah. If spending time in God's presence and being changed and touched by Him does not cause or compel us to go out into the world, then the phrase that comes to mind is "being so heavenly minded that we are of no earthly use!" Of course, our minds should be fixed on heaven, but our lives are lived in the reality of the here and now.

The resources here are partly organised according to the church's calendar, taking the changing seasons into account. It is not necessary to use them sequentially or at specific times. However, if you are using them to establish a rhythm or habit of regularly coming apart for reflection, there are enough resources to support you in doing so. By the time you have used them all, you will be well practised and more capable of sitting with scripture without additional aid.

The resources are designed with the expectation that participants will spend between 45 minutes and an hour in silence for each of the three sections. Of course, you may take longer if you wish, but I advise you not to shorten those periods of quiet, as this would reduce the opportunity to truly listen.

If you are planning to organise Quiet Days for a group, choose the resource that best fits your situation or the time of year. There are no strict rules about the order in which the resources can be used. Resources may also include helpful notes on additional ideas or focal points that could be created, but again, this is entirely optional and meant to inspire your own creativity.

I offer these resources humbly, praying they may benefit those who choose to use them, whether individually or in a group, knowing they have already served that purpose among those who attended days I led in the past.

Resource 1:
Advent 1: Obedience

Introduction

A focal point could be created with three pairs of shoes: a woman's pair, a man's pair and possibly a pair of baby shoes or booties. It would be helpful if the shoes showed signs of wear and tear rather than being pristine and highly polished. This would evoke a sense of journey and highlight the reality of hardship or challenges faced along the way.

Session 1: Travelling with Mary

Read Luke 1:26 – 38.

Nazareth was not a notable place; it was a city lacking any spotlight or expectations of anything.

Mary was an ordinary teenage girl with probably no great expectations beyond marriage. She was simply an adolescent going about her daily life. At the time the angel appeared, she also had no knowledge of Elizabeth's pregnancy.

An angel—what a shock! What did that even look like? Many artists with diverse perspectives have attempted to capture the image. It's important to note that the first thing the angel does is bring her reassurance in the midst of her fear. We are so familiar with the story and what is to come that we can overlook the emotion and the magnitude of the news

- for Mary

- for her community

- for her nation

- for the world

This message did not include any of her dreams or expectations, whether about the big picture or the personal ones.

This encounter did not last just a few seconds—the time it takes us to read it. This was a conversation. The Bible does not interpret pauses, emotions or even questions.

Mary's questions? How many did she have? We only know she asked the most obvious, practical one: "How can this be?"

The angel informs her about Elizabeth, acknowledging that it seems impossible, yet strengthens her faith by recognising that what is impossible can be overcome by God. How often does God remind us of something He has done to encourage us to believe and take a further step of faith?

"No word from God will ever fail" is an alternative translation of "Nothing is impossible with God". It prompted her to stop viewing things from her perspective, to cease seeing through the world's eyes and to start perceiving from God's perspective. She set aside her expectations, Joseph's expectations, others' expectations and cultural expectations, and she said "yes" to God.

"I am the Lord's servant," completely His and available to Him. At this moment, much remains unknown and uncertain, but every objection is set aside as she fully trusts herself to God.

During the days and months of Mary's pregnancy, she would witness many confirmations of what God had spoken and done amid pain, suffering and confusion. No wonder she treasured the words that had been spoken and the glimpses of God that she had witnessed along the way (Luke 2:19 and 51).

Obedience is not always an easy path, but it will bring moments of encounter. Hold onto those moments—remember them, reflect on them, treasure them.

Quiet Reflection

Reread Luke 1:26 – 38 several times. Does anything strike you afresh?

Try to appreciate the ordinariness of Mary's life, the emotion of the encounter and the magnitude of the change in circumstances that lies ahead.

The angel sees Mary for who she is—"highly favoured"—but she perceives herself as the Lord's servant. The two perspectives are not incompatible.

You will have your own view on how you see yourself, but consider asking God how He sees you today.

What is the Lord asking of you? How does Mary's example help you?

Read Luke 2:19 and 51. Do you need encouragement or confirmation to take a step of faith? Ask God to give you what you need in the days ahead.

Session 2: Travelling with Joseph

Read Matthew 1:18 – 25.

Joseph mainly remains in the background of the Christmas story. Culturally, this reflects a role reversal —Mary and the baby Jesus take centre stage while Joseph appears very much as a supporting character. But there are significant aspects of Joseph's life worth considering.

For Joseph, it is not an invitation to shape the process but to respond to what is already unfolding before him.

Firstly, he faces a significant dilemma: how would it have felt in the small community? For Joseph, the woman he loves is pregnant! She has seemingly betrayed his trust. He hears all the gossip, sees the knowing looks or hostile stares, but being a "righteous and godly man", he doesn't want to cause further hurt. We know the story well. How should we respond when faced with challenging situations?

That was Joseph's dilemma: should he walk away or cause a scene? The momentum was already there; he couldn't alter the situation, and he had already decided to walk away quietly.

The angel appears at that moment and shows him the bigger picture. Will he decide for his own sake or for the good of others? "What about me, or what about Mary? What will happen to her if I go?"

The journey is going to happen; will Joseph take part or take flight?

Secondly, Joseph acts as a facilitator. He plays a vital role in bringing things about.

Unlike Mary, Joseph has a dream in which an angel speaks to him (Matthew 2:19). He plays a background role, not a prominent one. Perhaps you are not one for the spotlight, but your faithfulness and obedience are crucial to the bigger picture. We honour those who serve in the background.

Joseph is the one entrusted with naming Jesus; he sets aside family tradition and is obedient to God.

Finally, Joseph exemplifies someone who accepts God's plan even when it is costly.

He displays wholehearted willingness; he doesn't hang about but gets straight on with it as soon as daylight breaks. True obedience and faith lead to immediate action. What is God asking you to do? It might not be centre stage, but it is deeply significant to Him.

Joseph embraces his role in God's plan, even though it is difficult.

Quiet Reflection

Reread Matthew 1:18 – 25 several times. Try to imagine yourself in Joseph's position.

Are you facing a dilemma? Ask God to show you His way and grant you peace as you make that decision.

Joseph's faithfulness and obedience are vital. Do you feel like you are "second fiddle", or perhaps you don't even feel you have made it to the orchestra? Those who work in the box office or clean the theatre are just as vital as those on the stage. Ask God to give you His perspective on your role in His big picture.

Joseph stepped into the limelight even as a support act. Is God asking you to step up? He will provide you with what you need, step by step, but are you willing to accept it?

Session 3: Travelling with Jesus

Read Phillipians 2:5 –11 and John 1:14.

The Christmas story as we know it mainly takes place in Nazareth and Bethlehem, but we are temporarily shifting it to heaven for a moment. As we read these verses in Philippians 2:5 – 11, we see Jesus, choosing not to grasp heaven or anything else, is relinquishing things that are His by right. He willingly lays down what is His own, not what He has earned or worked for, but what is His by right.

What does it mean to leave and not to grasp, to let go of comfort and familiarity, to give rather than receive?

What are we attempting to hold onto?

- Material security?

- Comfort? There is a mistaken belief that following God will keep us comfortable, which is not necessarily true at all. Conversely, we may have a distorted understanding and think that following God will lead to suffering. Both of these ideas are erroneous.

- What about my rights? I deserve...and we live with a sense of entitlement.

- Familiarity? We may hold onto what is safe, what is known.

- Reputation? We may cling to what will enhance our reputation or our status.

Jesus relinquished everything to become nothing. It was a deliberate choice that He made; it didn't just happen.

Where does it challenge us? Is your hand clenched or open? Do you hold things tightly or loosely? John 1:14 says, "The Word became flesh and made his dwelling among us." What does it mean to be someone who dwells in the neighbourhood? Jesus knows He is on a mission. He recognises that it is not an easy calling. Jesus's call is challenged in the wilderness three times by the temptation to choose His own way rather than God's way. Are you being tempted to take the easy option, or are you determined to keep your eyes fixed on Jesus?

Once more in Gethsemane, He struggles and wavers momentarily, but He keeps His gaze fixed on the Father and His purposes, guiding Him through the deepest pain imaginable, all the while knowing that the Father ultimately has led Him into wonderful, victorious, glorious wonder and salvation for all who will choose it.

The path of obedience may be utterly challenging, confusing and painful, but the journey walked with God is indescribably beautiful. His Spirit is our constant companion, guide and source of peace. The reward, therefore, is even more beyond description.

Quiet Reflection

Once more, take the time to reread the passages Phillipians 2: 5 – 11 and John 1:14. Then, take time to wonder, worship, praise and adore Jesus, thanking Him for His example of obedience and for all that He has accomplished for us. Finally, pray for the courage to continue walking obediently with Him, trusting that His Kingdom purposes will be realised in and through your life.

Resource 2
Advent 2:
The Gifts of the Magi

Read Matthew 2:1 – 12.

Introduction

A focal point for this day could be three boxes of varying sizes, wrapped to resemble gifts. Alternatively, you may consider different ways to represent these three gifts.

Our focus today is on the three gifts of the Magi—wise men, likely astrologers. They were probably quite wealthy to afford the lengthy and costly journey. They travelled to Jerusalem with the expectation of visiting a king in a palace.

Whoever they were, they were significant individuals who clearly recognised the importance of this birth.

Regardless of their background, they were undoubtedly spiritually aware, and whether they recognised it or not, their gifts conveyed a potent, prophetic message. This serves as a reminder that God can use anyone, not solely those who believe they know Him or heed His voice.

Session 1: Gold

Gold—a gift fit for a king. Precious, costly and highly valued. There is something rather incongruous about such a gift being given in such humble surroundings, probably not still in the cave or stable (if that is even where they were originally) but more likely staying with distant relatives in a place of relative poverty.

I have a slightly mischievous sense of curiosity, which makes me wonder whether the Magi ever doubted what they were doing. They expected a king in a palace, not a peasant family hiding in a stable or staying in what would be the equivalent of a cheap motel. Do we ever question what God asks of us? Especially when it takes us to people or places we never imagined?

Gold, regardless of the circumstances, was a gift for a king.

The Queen of Sheba presented Solomon, in all his splendour, with numerous gifts, including 120 talents of gold, along with large quantities of spices and precious stones, which probably also included frankincense and myrrh.

Interestingly, when consulted by Herod, the priests and experts of the law only mentioned the first part of the prophecy from Micah. They quoted from Micah 5:2: "But you, Bethlehem Ephrathah, though you are small among the clans of Judah, out of you will come for me one who will be ruler over Israel."

Perhaps because they valued their lives and feared the wrath of Herod, they stopped short of Micah 5:4 – 5, which speaks of the majesty of Jesus reaching to the ends of the earth. I wonder if we ever stop short of the complete truth because we fear the reaction of others?

These wise men recognised Jesus as royalty, and despite His surroundings, they knelt and worshipped Him. What was it about His very presence that compelled them to bow down?

We reflect on the prophecies concerning Jesus; Isaiah contains numerous examples, as do many of the Old Testament prophets. Likewise, King David recognised that he was a monarch under the authority of the King of Kings, as embodied in Jesus.

Zechariah speaks of Jesus, "See your king comes to you, righteous and victorious, lowly and riding on a donkey" (Zechariah 9:9).

But in scripture, we also look forward. Revelation 17:14 and Revelation 19:16 speak of the time when He will reign triumphant, glorious in heavenly splendour.

As we enter a time of quiet, the question is this: have we become so familiar with the gentle Jesus, riding on a donkey, Jesus the man, that we have lost perspective on His Majesty? His Holiness? His Almighty-ness?

In the dramatic book of Esther, we read that Queen Esther feared death by stepping into the presence of the King unbidden, despite being the Queen. Thanks be to God, we need not fear death—quite the opposite; however, let us take some time to be in reverence and awe. Encountering a king would be an incredible experience, but meeting the King of All Kings will be beyond words.

Quiet Reflection

Take time to quietly worship the King of Kings.

Read and reflect on Psalm 47. What does it mean to you personally that "God is seated on his holy throne?" (Psalm 47:8).

Is there any area of your life that is not submitted to His Kingship?

You may like to listen to the worship song 'King of Kings, Majesty'.

Session 2: Frankincense

Frankincense is a shimmering, aromatic resin obtained by making deep cuts in the bark of a specific tree. By splitting the word, "frank" means free, referring to how it smokes freely and intensely when burnt.

Read Song of Songs 3:6: "Who is this coming up from the wilderness like a column of smoke, perfumed with myrrh and incense made from all the spices of the merchant?" And

Malachi 1:11: "My name will be great among the nations, from where the sun rises to where it sets. In every place incense and pure offerings will be brought to me." This gift was a worthy offering and the fulfilment of prophecy. The Old Testament reveals the connection between frankincense and the priestly role. Exodus 30:34 – 37 states the following: "Then the Lord said to Moses, 'Take fragrant spices—gum resin, onycha and galbanum—and pure frankincense, all in equal amounts, and make a fragrant blend of incense, the work of a perfumer. It is to be salted and pure and sacred. Grind some of it to powder and place it in front of the ark of the covenant law in the tent of meeting, where I will meet with you. It shall be most holy to you. Do not make any incense with this formula for yourselves; consider it holy to the Lord.'"

It was a sacred substance and emitted a scent that signified the presence of God meeting with man. What more fitting gift to indicate that Jesus was holy and divine? God meeting man, God becoming man.

Phillipians 2:6 – 8 says of Jesus, "Who, being in very nature God, did not consider equality with God something to be used to his own advantage; rather, he made himself nothing by taking the very nature of a servant, being made in human likeness. And being found in appearance as a man, he humbled himself by becoming obedient to death—even death on a cross!" Leviticus 2:1 tells us that incense was poured out on the grain offering, making something that was ordinary and acceptable offering, signifying its holiness; in the same way, this gift of frankincense signified the holiness of the infant Jesus. The priest was the one who represented humanity to God and God to humanity, which is, of course, what Jesus did and continues to do for us.

Psalm 141:2 says, "May my prayer be set before you like incense; may the lifting up of my hands be like the evening sacrifice." Luke 1:10 says, "And when the time for burning incense came, all the assembled worshippers were praying outside" (As Zachariah enters the Holy of Holies).

Reflecting on the past, we can identify numerous references that illustrate the prophetic nature of this gift. As we look to the future, we continue to see this connection of God meeting mankind through the intimacy of prayer.

As stated in Revelation 5:8 and 8:3, our prayers are like incense rising to heaven—what an inspiring thought! This should encourage us, especially in those moments when we find it difficult to pray. God delights in hearing our prayers.

Romans 8:34 states, "Who then is the one who condemns? No one. Christ Jesus who died—more than that, who was raised to life—is at the right hand of God and is also interceding for us." Jesus continues to intercede on our behalf. He stands before the Father on behalf of you, me and all mankind.

Listen closely. What is He saying to the Father about you? How does the Father respond to Him? When we think about prayer, what comes to mind? Usually, we imagine words, needs or perhaps unanswered prayers, but prayer encompasses so much more than that. It is a conversation. We have one mouth and two ears, which suggests that we should listen more than we speak. Does this reflect the prayers we are accustomed to? Do we listen to what our Holy God says when we converse with Him about the issues that weigh on our hearts? I remember listening to a well-known speaker recount how the Lord revealed to her that she was praying the wrong prayer. She recalled how a member of her family lost their job and how she had prayed fervently for them to find something suitable. However, despite all her prayers, the family continued to face increasing financial difficulties until they eventually lost their home and had to move in with her and her husband. She was very cross with God and one day shouted at Him, "Why are you not answering my prayers?" And she said, as clearly as anything, she heard Him respond, "Because you are praying the wrong prayer." Not surprisingly, this stopped her in her tracks. "What should I be praying?" she asked, and very gently and clearly, He showed her that His purposes for the family were for them to learn certain things, including a new reliance on God. Humbled, she adjusted her prayers to align with God's purposes, and as she did so, she witnessed changes taking place. Not long after that, they also found new employment. It is a lesson that I have never forgotten. Sadly, most of us, myself included, often expect answers to manifest as actions. When God acts, I know He has responded. Can we truly presume to tell our Holy God what to do? Or should we seek guidance from Jesus, the Great Intercessor, about what He is praying? What weighs on His heart for this or that situation?

Quiet Reflection

You may want to take a moment to reflect on Jesus, the Priest, the Intercessor, speaking to God the Father. What is He praying?

Your prayers are like incense rising up in heaven (Revelation 5:8 and 8:3). How does that make you feel?

Have you been struggling with prayer? Invite the Holy Spirit to assist you.

You may like to use the Taizé chant, 'Oh Lord, hear my prayer.'

Session 3: Myrrh

Myrrh is a perfume, incense and medicine, also harvested from the bark of a tree, similar to frankincense. It is mentioned 156 times in the Bible.

In Genesis 37:25, we read that the caravan of traders who purchased Joseph from his brothers was carrying myrrh. In Esther 2:12, we learn that Esther underwent six months of beauty treatments with oil of myrrh.

Exodus 30:23 – 29 discusses the oil of holy anointing. The primary ingredient was myrrh, and its purpose was to designate it as divine. Everything in the temple was saturated with this particular fragrance to mark it as holy to the Lord. Smells can be very evocative. Have you ever detected a smell, whether pleasant or unpleasant, that has transported you to another time and place? It conjures memories of an event or a person. This myrrh-based oil was similar—it was telling people, "Remember this is holy!"

Therefore, the initial prophetic declaration of this gift also serves to remind us of Jesus's holiness. 1 Peter 2:22 states, "He committed no sin, and no deceit was found in his mouth."

The second function of myrrh is as a fragrance worthy of a king. Psalms 45:8 – 9 say, "All your robes are fragrant with myrrh and aloes and cassia; from palaces adorned with ivory, the music of the strings makes you glad. Daughters of kings are among your honoured women; at your right hand is the royal bride in gold of Ophir." This was a royal wedding song but also a foreshadowing of Jesus (which means we are the bride dressed in gold!). Song of Songs 3:6 states, "Who is this coming up from the wilderness like a column of smoke, perfumed with myrrh and incense, made from all the spices of the merchant?" And Song of Songs 5:5 says, "I arose to open for my beloved, and my hands dripped with myrrh, my fingers with flowing myrrh, on the handles of the bolt."

We could explore many other references that discuss the link between myrrh and love, intimacy, joy and celebration.

We may rush so rapidly to its third meaning, which is one of bitterness and death, that we may overlook the true depth and significance of this third prophetic gift.

Take some time to marvel at God's love and desire for intimacy with us and His joy in relationship with us. This is truly awe-inspiring, but it does lead us to its third prophetic function.

In Mark 15:23, it is noted that it was offered as a painkiller while Jesus hung on the cross, but he did not accept it.

John 19:39 – 40 speaks of a phenomenal amount used to anoint Jesus's body. "Nicodemus brought a mixture of myrrh and aloes, about seventy-five pounds. Taking Jesus's body, the two of them wrapped it, with the spices, in strips of linen. This was in accordance with Jewish burial customs." Imagine the expense and logistics of handling approximately 34 kilograms. Consider the potency of the fragrance, and reflect on the power of holiness, love and the cost of suffering.

This demonstrates how much Jesus loves us—extravagantly, passionately, righteously, even to death. Why would we ever doubt or hold back in our response?

Quiet Reflection

Which of these three aspects—holiness, intimacy, or suffering—touches or surprises you the most? Take time to reflect on that aspect and perhaps revisit the scriptures we examined:

Holiness: Exodus 30:23 – 29

Intimacy: Song of Songs 3:6 and 5:5

Suffering: any of the crucifixion passages

What is your heartfelt response?

MARGARET WOODING JONES

Resource 3
Lent 1: Last Words

Introduction

Lent is a significant time for personal reflection, when we take the opportunity to examine our lives and our journey with the Lord more closely. In this reflection, we will consider words spoken by Jesus as He prepared Himself, and more specifically, as He instructed His disciples about the events that were about to unfold in the Easter story.

Last words are always significant words—the words you want someone to remember. They are carefully considered, heartfelt words, words to be treasured, words we ponder and reflect upon. I remember many years ago when our family was about to go on an extended visit to South America; my in-laws had taken us to the airport to see us off. As we moved through the departure hall, heading for security, our four-year-old son turned around and shouted at the top of his voice, "I love you Granny!" Needless to say, many eyes were moistened, but for him, it was the most important thing he wanted his granny to remember.

Session 1: Don't Be Troubled

John 14:1 says, "Do not let your hearts be troubled. You believe in God; believe also in me." The disciples had been with Jesus for three years. They had given up their businesses and livelihoods to travel with Him and learn from Him.

Jesus knew what lay ahead, and He had complete confidence in His Father. Although He had warned the disciples, He also understood that their lives would be shaken by the events of the coming days. He was aware of the questions that would arise in their hearts.

"What have we done?" "Did we fail Him?" "Was this guy for real, or have we been totally deceived?" "Am I next?" All of these are understandable; it is not too difficult for us to imagine what the disciples would have been feeling and thinking in the days to come. Jesus's words to them are, "Do not let your hearts be troubled. You believe in God; believe also in me" (John 14:1). You can almost feel the comforting tone in His words.

Not one of them, possibly not even John, was able to walk through the following days without succumbing to fear; all of them deserted Jesus in the Garden of Gethsemane. They slept in His greatest hour of need; they abandoned Him to the soldiers, and even though Peter followed at a distance, he too succumbed to fear. He sought self-preservation by denying that he knew Jesus. We cannot blame or judge them but must accept that we, too, give in to fear time and again.

Jesus had previously asked, "Who of you by worrying can add a single hour to your life?" (Luke 12:25). In fact, quite the reverse is true: excessive worry may well shorten our lives. Jesus addresses our fears too. He says, "Do not let your hearts be troubled. You believe in God; believe also in me" (John 14:1).

During your quiet time, ask God, "Is there any situation that makes me fearful?". Perhaps you already know. You might find it helpful to write a list of your fears; maybe there is just one, or perhaps a whole page full. Work through them one at a time, choosing to give each one to Him. You might like to imagine wrapping them up or placing them in a bin bag before handing them over to Him. It could be a person you are concerned about; you might want to picture holding their hand, guiding them to Jesus and placing their hand in His (similar to the father of the bride).

Your fears might be deep-seated, unspoken worries like "Am I really saved?" or "Does Jesus really love me?"

Whatever the fear, as you "hand it over", ask Jesus if there is a word or scripture to hold onto the next time that same fear arises within you. Instead of entertaining the fear, meditate on the word or scripture and remind the enemy that Jesus now holds that fear, not you.

Quiet Reflection

Reread John 14:1 several times. What does trusting God actually look like? Is there any area of disquiet or trouble that comes to your mind? Talk to the Lord about it. What do you need to entrust to Him?

As you reflect on the different disciples in this Easter story, do any responses stand out to you? Bring these to Jesus and ask Him to guide you on how you might respond differently.

Session 2: Abide in Me

It's not about doing; it's about being. A branch doesn't strive to be part of a tree; it simply is.

Read John 15:1 –5.

What does "being in Christ" mean? It's not about achievement or spiritual intelligence; it's about being still in Him, resting in Him, being enveloped in His love—not because we are good enough but simply because He loves us. We are His creation, the apple of His eye and children of a loving Heavenly Father. It is not something we earn or work for; it is something we receive. Being "in Christ" is a gift.

Life knocks us down—emotionally, physically, materially and even spiritually. At best, we are bumped and bruised; at worst, we are maimed and shredded. We have all experienced it in one way or another.

Now may be the season for pruning: removing unnecessary growth and trimming fruitful branches, always with the aim of creating something stronger and even more productive. The fruitful branch is not lost; it must look to the tree, the trunk and the roots for all the goodness and nutrients it needs for new growth. I'm not very skilled at pruning; I'm still learning, and sometimes I cut off the wrong part. Father God is not like that—He is the expert pruner; He knows exactly what is needed.

Jesus said earlier in John 10:10, "I have come that they may have life, and have it to the full." Now He's speaking about being pruned. It doesn't seem like the fullness of life when we are pruned, yet it is always to prepare us for greater fruitfulness.

Jesus knew the disciples were about to face their greatest pruning. Their lives were set to be utterly disorientating; far from being celebrated close friends of Jesus, they would soon find themselves cowering in fear for their lives, feeling cut off from Jesus and their heads filled with doubts and questions. This would be followed by the most extraordinary outpouring and a time of fruitfulness, which we read about in Acts.

However, Jesus is not focusing on the pruning or the fruitfulness; His recurring message throughout this passage is remain in me; abide in me.

Fruitfulness will be mostly external and visible— aspects we observe in one another. We cannot see what happens underground or inside the trunk of a tree; it remains hidden. Abiding or remaining is also an unseen, internal process; it takes place in the heart, where only the Lord can see. What does it mean for you to abide in Jesus? We will now take some time to be quiet and reflect on these questions. Are you genuinely abiding, drawing your strength from Him, whether in a season of pruning or a fruitful season? What does abiding look like in your life? Are there changes you need to make to fully abide? Choosing to be here today is a sign of that desire, but do you need to abide more?

Quiet Reflection

Reread John 15:1 – 5 several times. Does anything strike you particularly? Ask God to show you why this is important for you.

Other questions you may like to consider:

What does it mean for me to abide in Jesus? What does this look like in my life?

Am I genuinely drawing my strength from him, whether during a period of pruning or a season of fruitfulness?

Are there changes I need to make to fully abide?

Session 3: Unless I Go

Jesus said, "Unless I go away, the Advocate will not come to you" (John 16:7). The Advocate, the Counsellor, the Comforter, the speaker of truth—these are the very things we have been seeking today. He is the Comforter of our souls—when we are frightened or anxious, He brings comfort and reassurance. When we have been deceived into unbelief, if we allow Him, the Spirit will speak truth into our lives. He will nourish us with good things, like sap in the tree.

As we contemplate the Holy Spirit, Romans 8:11 is enlightening: "And if the Spirit of him who raised Jesus from the dead is living in you, he who raised Christ from the dead will also give life to your mortal bodies because of his Spirit who lives in you."

This echoes another statement made by Jesus: "I have come that they may have life, and have it to the full" (John 10:10).

This occurs as Jesus speaks about being the Good Shepherd, with the sheep recognising, hearing and obeying His voice. "If you know Me, listen to Me, and follow Me, you will experience the fullness of life." What does fullness look like? Not necessarily the absence of trouble, as we considered regarding the vine, but fullness is living in the certain assurance that our lives are derived from Him, not from anything else.

It's a beautiful passage, but it carries many warnings. The first part of John 10:10 states "The thief comes only to kill, steal and destroy." The enemy believed he had ultimately killed, stolen and destroyed Jesus on the cross. However, this is not so; he still seeks to kill, steal and destroy Jesus's followers, and that includes you and me. As we conclude our time today and reflect on these two passages, we might want to ask, "Do I genuinely believe that the Spirit who raised Christ Jesus from the dead is living and active in me? If so, what difference does He make to the lives of those around me?" And "Am I living in the fullness of life that Christ has won for me? And if not, why not? What is holding me back or robbing me?"

Quiet Reflection

Reread each of the passages several times: Romans 8:11 and John 10:10.

Ask God to refill and refresh you with a sense of His Holy Spirit in you.

Prayerfully consider the following questions and write down your thoughts.

Do I truly believe that the Spirit who raised Christ Jesus from the dead is living and active within me? If so, what difference does He make to me and the lives of those around me?

Am I living in the fullness of life that Christ has won for me? If not, what is holding me back or robbing me?

Note down anything you resolve to do to live life differently—remember, it may be more about "being" than "doing".

Resource 4

Lent 2: The Temptations of Jesus

Read Matthew 4: 1 – 11.

Session 1: Making Sacrifices

Lent is traditionally considered a time for fasting. Throughout the centuries, Christians have used this period to abstain from things, whether that be a complete food fast or items such as fresh eggs, meat, chocolate or, nowadays, perhaps social media. All are given up with the intention of getting closer to God, to give more time to seek His face and to let Him search our hearts.

Jesus, too, felt this need—not to give up chocolate but to renounce everything: food, the comforts of home and the company of others—for a wild, off-grid camping trip. He didn't rest by a beautiful oasis but instead chose a desolate place, one devoid of distractions.

It prompts the questions, "What are we prepared to sacrifice to draw closer to God? Are there times and seasons when God calls us away to gain our complete attention?"

Matthew states that Jesus was led by the Spirit to be tempted. Perhaps He was, but I think it is far more probable that the temptations arose as a consequence of His fasting. I love Matthew's understated way of saying that having not eaten for 40 days, He was hungry! Following such an extreme fast, Jesus would have been physically, mentally and emotionally depleted, and it is in that moment that He is tempted.

I sometimes wonder whether our illustrated children's Bibles are always helpful, depicting Satan as something between a beast and a human with horns, hairy red skin and a toasting fork. He may have appeared in person or, like us, the temptations may have been just thoughts crossing Jesus's mind. Either way, Jesus must have spoken about these events so that Matthew, Mark and Luke were able to record what happened since none of them were actually there.

In this first session, we will concentrate on the first temptation. "After fasting forty days and forty nights, he was hungry. The tempter came to him and said, 'If you are the Son of God, tell these stones to become bread.' Jesus answered, 'It is written: 'Man shall not live on bread alone, but on every word that comes from the mouth of God''" (Matthew 4:2 – 4).

Satan seeks to sow a seed of doubt in Jesus's mind, and he will employ the same tactic on us as well. There is one small word; it's only two letters, yet it makes a world of difference.

"If you are the Son of God." Imagine the statement without the "if". "You are the Son of God", which Satan absolutely knows to be true, and Jesus does too. Had Satan said that, Jesus might have responded with "You're right, I am the Son of God. Therefore, I don't need to prove it." But Satan tries to needle Him with this doubt of "if".

Nor does Jesus say, "Actually, I am the Son of God; I don't need to eat bread."

Rather than affirm that He is God, Jesus instead points to His humanity. At the very moment when He is being challenged about His divinity, He directs attention to His humanity: "Man does not live by bread alone, but every word that proceeds from the mouth of the Father" (Matthew 4:4).

Two thoughts come to mind here. Firstly, the verse that says Jesus "did not consider equality with God something to be used to his own advantage; rather, he made himself nothing by taking the very nature of a servant being made in human likeness" (Phillippians 2:6 – 8). This was a powerful way for Jesus to identify with us, to be like us and to not hold up the God card. He gives us a model of how we too can overcome the tempter.

The second point involves responding with the opposite spirit. When we are tempted or provoked by others, it is crucial to reply in the opposite spirit to help defuse the situation.

What Satan was really attempting was to tempt Jesus into proving Himself to be God. Jesus effectively answers him, "I am a man", and He goes on to say, "But even so, my needs are not as important as hearing from God." Wow! What a victory! Satan cannot counter the truth.

As we come to a time of reflection, which "ifs" do you need to knock on the head? What seeds of doubt has Satan planted in your mind?

If God has called me, then I should...

If I'm a child of God then I shouldn't...

If I were a better person...

If, if, if.

Remove the "if" and observe what remains. "If you are the Son of God" becomes "you are the Son of God" or "if God has called me" turns into "God has called me." This shift offers a different perspective and may help you redirect your focus from yourself to the One who has called you.

An "if" is always followed by a "then". For Jesus, the "then" He was tempted by was "look after yourself, meet your own needs". It may be the "then" that warrants challenge and needs to be viewed from God's perspective.

During this first time of reflection, remain still and quiet and ask God to reveal the doubts you have been listening to.

Quiet Reflection

Reread Matthew 4:2 – 4 several times and see what God might show you.

Ask him to indicate whether there are any doubts you might have been listening to.

Remove the "if" and observe what remains.

You might like to consider what it means to come with the opposite spirit. When I am tempted, what is the contrary? How do I redirect the focus from myself to God's purpose?

Session 2: Temptation

Read Matthew 4:5-7.

Many years ago, I was struck by Satan's grasp of scripture and his ability to quote it. At the time, I had to look up and see where this came from, and as I read Psalm 91, I thought, "No wonder the enemy of our souls has checked this Psalm out!"

It's like Father's battle plan, only it's not a secret. At that point, I decided I would read it every day during Lent and commit it to memory. Personally, I find it very challenging to learn scripture by heart; it requires significant discipline from me. So each day, I asked my daughter to test me—a great way to help get scripture into your children's hearts too! As Lent went on, I don't believe there was a day I didn't share a verse or two with someone. Not randomly, but intentionally and specifically. It's a psalm that seems to connect with many situations. It is always relevant and fresh; it is the living Word! Now, turn to Psalm 91 and read it together.

This psalm is incredibly rich; we could easily spend the whole day exploring it. Verses 2, 4, 9, 10 and 14 specifically speak powerfully of God's protection.

But here are other "ifs" and "thens", this time revealing the consequences of following God's ways.

"Whoever dwells in the shelter of the Most High will rest in the shadow of the Almighty" (Psalm 91:1) could be paraphrased as "If you dwell in the shelter of the Most High, then you will rest in the shadow of the Almighty."

"If you say 'The Lord is my refuge' and you make the Most High your dwelling, [then] no harm will overtake you" (Psalm 91:9).

And herein lies a problem: Christians do suffer. Terrible things happen to Christians. Some of the most joy-filled and faithful souls endure horrendous persecution, illness or family tragedy.

We may quote this psalm back to Him and say, "You didn't do it for me," and sadly, I know some who have given up their faith in God due to loss or tragedy. However, God does not abandon His people. Verses 14 and 15 state, "'Because he loves me,' says the Lord, 'I will rescue him; I will protect him, for he acknowledges my name. He will call on me, and I will answer him; I will be with him in trouble, I will deliver him and honour him.'" This reminds me of Jesus saying, "In this world you will have trouble. But take heart! I have overcome the world" (John 16:33).

This psalm should be seen as a spiritual image rather than just a commentary on our physical, human conditions. If we are hidden in God and pressed into Him as tightly as possible, we may face incredible difficulties; however, God's presence will stay with us and often shine through for others to observe.

What was happening here with Jesus in the wilderness was that Satan, although correctly quoting scripture, was attempting to tempt Jesus to step out from underneath the covering of God, to step away from His presence and take a step towards Satan. This was another attempt to get Jesus to prove that He was God.

There are times when God calls us to step out in faith, and indeed, moments when it feels like stepping off a cliff. If God is guiding you, you will certainly experience His protection and rescue. I remember telling a friend that when my husband and I had just taken a huge step of faith, it felt as though we had just stepped off a cliff. He said, "Yes, but God will give you the wings to fly." And that, in due course, became our testimony.

Satan's deception sought to draw Jesus away from God, a tactic he continues to employ today. Jesus sees straight through it and replies with scripture, saying, "Do not put the Lord you God to the test" (Deuteronomy 6:16). A brief aside: there is a significant difference between putting God to the test and testing God's Word. Testing God would be like putting your hand in the fire to see if you get burnt—a completely pointless exercise. Testing God's Word is a completely different matter; it's us saying, "I think you're saying this, but I'm not sure." An obvious example would be Gideon and the two fleeces (Judges 6:36 – 40).

So, are there any ways that Satan might lead you to step away from the protective care of God and take a step closer to him? It may not be as dramatic as stepping off the temple, but the consequences could be just as catastrophic.

Quiet Reflection

Use Psalm 91 as a guide for meditation. Read it slowly several times; then observe what captures your attention most. Focus on that.

Alternatively, you might consider asking God to reveal any ways in which you may be drawn away from Him. What scripture could assist you in countering the enemy's tactics?

Session 3: Resisting the Enemy

Read Matthew 4:8 – 11. There are times when, in desperation, Satan oversteps the mark. This is one of them. It may seem absurd to us that, having failed to persuade Jesus first to prove His divinity and then to test God's care and faithfulness, he should now try to get Jesus to worship him. How outrageous!

And yet, that may also be a familiar pattern in our own lives or among those we love. It begins with doubting, for instance, our true worth, especially when we are experiencing suffering. Then, in that moment of doubt, we might try to test God to see whether what He says is true rather than living by faith. Ultimately, after doubting God's Word to us, we may think it is all a waste of time or a delusion and walk away from Him, feeling disappointed and hurt. Some of the hardest hearts may be those who have had an experience of God but have turned away and become completely resistant to hearing the truth. It's heartbreaking, but it happens, and Satan rejoices at the thought.

Jesus is unequivocal in His response: "Away from me, Satan!" (Matthew 4:10). He then turns directly to the first commandment, fixing His own and Satan's eyes steadily on God.

There are times when we must be radical about temptation and about sin should we fall into it. Jesus said something seemingly outrageous in the Sermon on the Mount. "If your right eye causes you to stumble, gouge it out and throw it away. It is better for you to lose one part of your body than for your whole body to be thrown into hell. And if your right hand causes you to stumble, cut it off and throw it away. It is better for you to lose one part of your body than for your whole body to go into hell" (Matthew 5:29 – 30). I'm not sure He was advocating physical self-harm, but He was saying, "Be absolutely ruthless and radical" when it comes to being drawn away from God's ways. Let's face it; we all fail and need help from time to time.

Jesus remained utterly resolute throughout His testing, and so can we, provided we stay close to Him.

James, in his Epistle, gives us a clue as to how. "Consider it pure joy, my brothers and sisters, whenever you face trials of many kinds, because you know that the testing of your faith produces perseverance. Let perseverance finish its work so that you may be mature and complete, not lacking anything" (James 1:2 – 4).

Joy isn't the first thing that may come to mind when you are being tested, but isn't that the "coming in the opposite spirit" we considered earlier? That joy isn't something we must muster up ourselves, which at best will only produce a fake smile while we tremble inwardly. The joy James speaks of is found only in the company of Jesus: "You will fill me with joy in your presence" (Psalm 16:11). This doesn't mean we are happy about our trials—far from it. To persevere means to press even more into God, knowing that as we come through, our faith will be even stronger.

Having stood His ground, Jesus is left alone by Satan (for a while), and angels come to attend to Him. What might that have looked like? We can't really know for certain, but it seems like a tremendous sigh of relief and a sense of peace descending upon Him from the heavenly realms.

When we face times of trial, whatever they may look like, it is beneficial to step back and rest for a while, allowing ourselves time to recover and reflect, letting God minister to us in whichever way He chooses.

As we conclude this time, let's reflect on the trials we have faced and what we might learn from them, thanking God for His presence with us.

Quiet Reflection

Reread Matthew 4:8 – 11, meditating on the words.

What confidence does Jesus's steadfastness inspire in you?

Do you need to take any radical action to avert Satan's activity or the consequences of failure? How might you achieve that? Don't feel afraid or ashamed to seek help.

Have you experienced a period of testing? Were you able to count it all joy?

Resource 5

Holy Week: Four Men Who Bore Crosses

Introduction

There is an abundance of material here and much to contemplate, so these reflections could be used daily throughout Holy Week rather than all at once in a single day. They were originally written and shared online during lockdown for Holy Week, with the fourth session being used on Good Friday.

An obvious focal point would be to use a simple wooden cross, preferably rough and splintered.

Session 1: Simon of Cyrene

Firstly, we will examine Simon of Cyrene. You will find one sentence in each of the Gospels of Matthew, Mark and Luke but none at all in John—a brief sentence in which a man is named and then goes down in history.

He may have had only a brief appearance, but for him, this could very well have been an utterly life-changing moment. In Matthew 27:32, we read, "As they were going out, they met a man from Cyrene, named Simon, and they forced him to carry the cross." Mark 15:21 states, "A certain man from Cyrene,

Simon, the father of Alexander and Rufus, was passing by on his way in from the country, and they forced him to carry the cross."

And in Luke 23:26 similarly, we read, "As the soldiers led him away, they seized Simon from Cyrene, who was on his way in from the country, and put the cross on him and made him carry it behind Jesus."

That's not much to go on. We know he was a visitor to Jerusalem, coming from Cyrene, a major city in Libya. It seems his sons were known to the readers of Mark's Gospel, possibly the church in Rome. Likely, Simon was a Jew who had travelled to Jerusalem to celebrate the Passover, but that remains largely speculative.

The key details indicate that a man named Simon from Cyrene was forced by the soldiers to carry the crossbar, as Jesus was too weakened from the flogging He had endured to bear it Himself. We can also assume that, at some point, his own family came to believe in Jesus, perhaps because of this very encounter.

Imagine yourself for a moment visiting the Holy City, preparing to celebrate one of the most precious and exhilarating feasts, probably with family in tow, when suddenly you find yourself caught up in a riot. People are shouting abuse, and soldiers march along, adding their shouts and insults both to the victims and likely to the passers-by as well. Have you pressed forward to see what is happening, or are you cowering back, attempting to shield your family from the chaos around you? Whatever the circumstances, you suddenly realise that the shouting is directed at you. You are grabbed and pulled forward, forced to carry the crossbar of a man who is so bloodied and weakened that he has stumbled and is now lying face down in the dirt.

You lift the splintered wood from him and press your shoulder against it, feeling the wetness of his sweat and blood soaking into your own clothes. The soldier pulls this man to his feet, and as he struggles to stand. Your eyes meet...a look you will never forget for as long as you live. Those eyes are so filled with pain, a man who has endured so much and yet there is something else there too. Is it love? Is it sympathy? Is it gratitude? Those eyes are so full; they are kind and compassionate, and at the same time, this man seems to look into your very soul.

At what point did Simon realise who this Jesus was? We have no idea. Perhaps he knew from the start. Maybe he watched as He was raised onto the cross, heard what He said and listened to Him declare forgiveness to those who would listen and to those who would not. Perhaps he saw His death. Maybe he was already known to the disciples or perhaps he wasn't. We simply do not know.

But we can surely assume that he was never the same again. Can you imagine how he felt, carrying the very item that Jesus, the Son of God, had carried and was then nailed to? The torn emotions and tangled thoughts of being screamed at by the domineering soldiers, with no choice but to comply.

There may have been terror and guilt, along with a feeling of complete helplessness. He, too, was at the merciless hands of the Roman soldiers.

I wonder whether he felt a sense of guilt for helping in Jesus's death, even though he had no choice. This made me think that each of us bear that same guilt, not because we carried that crossbar, but because of our own guilt and sin—both the actions undertaken knowingly and willingly those committed without choice. For example, being unintentionally part of wider societal sin, such as unintended environmental harm, although there are many other examples.

We cannot know what interactions took place between Jesus and Simon, but we are certain that Jesus understood Simon's heart. Simon may have witnessed Jesus on the cross and heard His declaration of forgiveness. As we enter this initial period of silence, you may wish to reflect more deeply on the scene surrounding Simon of Cyrene, or consider any ways in which you might have been complicit in Jesus's crucifixion.

Quiet Reflection

Read Matthew 27:32, Mark 15:21 and Luke 23:26.

As you reread one of these passages and try to imagine the noise, the smells and the atmosphere, are you able to put yourself in Simon's place? How does this make you feel? Can you see Jesus in this scenario? The soldiers would likely have forbidden any conversation, but what do you see? What would you say to Jesus?

Take some time now to reflect on how you may have been complicit in Jesus's crucifixion.

When have you felt powerless to change anything? Perhaps an injustice or an addictive behaviour. Use this opportunity to speak to Jesus about it now and, like Simon, hear Him say, "Father, forgive them, they know not what they do."

Session 2: The Unrepentant Criminal

Read Matthew 27: 38 – 44, Mark 15: 27 – 32 and Luke 23: 32 – 39.

As we consider the second man mentioned in the Gospels, who carried his own cross and was cruelly nailed to it just as Jesus was, this perhaps represents the most challenging situation for us to reflect upon.

In the first session, we considered Simon of Cyrene, an innocent bystander who was compelled to carry the cross for Jesus. Now, we are considering a man who, as far as we know, was justly tried, found guilty and sentenced to crucifixion for his actions.

All four Gospels tell us that there were two rebels or robbers who were crucified with Him and that they also heaped insults on Him. Jesus was mocked and jeered by many who had gathered to witness this most gruesome spectacle of death. Although all the

Gospels record that they both joined in the abuse, only Luke mentions that one later experienced a change of heart. We will examine him next but for now, we are focusing on the one who did not seem to change at all.

This is a difficult story because it lacks a happy or satisfying outcome. As far as we know, he died with a hardened heart and an angry disposition, jeering at Jesus and suggesting that Jesus should save not only Himself but him as well.

It is an extremely difficult story because this criminal was blind to the fact that the very One who could save him was hanging there with His arms stretched wide open right beside him. Salvation was so close and yet so far. It is a true saying that there are none so blind as those who will not see. Understanding cannot be forced upon someone who chooses to be ignorant; insight cannot be given to someone who appears incapable of comprehending.

Just a few days earlier, as Jesus was entering the city of Jerusalem from the Mount of Olives, He wept over the city and its people, saying, "If you, even, you, had only known on this day what would bring you peace —but now it is hidden from your eyes" (Luke 19:42). I am certain that Jesus's grief was just as real for this one man, so near and yet so far away. There is a common saying that goes, "Hurt people, hurt people." What has made this man so angry, so bitter? Of course we have no idea, but he was not born like that. At some point in his life, events happened or circumstances arose that caused him grief and hardship. No child dreams of becoming a criminal one day, yet somewhere along the way, possibly through injustice and poverty, or perhaps through harmful influences or broken relationships, his dreams were lost, and he became hardened and hurtful.

There had been many people Jesus had encountered whose lives had been broken and whose hopes had been dashed; yet just one word, one conversation, one touch from Jesus had transformed them. Yet here was this man, right beside Him, and he missed it.

As we take some time now for quiet reflection, there may be various ways to respond to this story. Consider the options below and see which resonates with you most strongly.

Quiet Reflection

Read Matthew 27: 38 – 44, Mark 15: 27 – 32 and Luke 23: 32 – 39.

Reflect on one of these passages, envisioning the sights and sounds of the events occurring. Pay special attention to the unrepentant criminal.

You might want to reflect on your own life. Is there some unhealed hurt that continues to cause you to react poorly to others? Perhaps it only surfaces occasionally, but you know it is still present. Now could be an excellent time to allow Jesus to touch that and grant you peace. Perhaps someone, in their pain, lashes out—someone who has hurt you or continues to do so through their words or behaviour. Ask Jesus to help you see them as He sees them and, like Jesus, forgive them for they may not realise what they are truly doing.

Much like Jesus, you might feel compelled to weep for those you know and love—whether individuals, nations or communities—that remain unaware of who Jesus is and what He can truly offer them. Take time to cry out in prayer for their turning and salvation, in contrast to this man who bore his cross and endured his punishment alone.

Session 3: The Other Criminal

Read Luke 23:39 – 43.

We have considered Simon of Cyrene, who had the cross thrust upon him; we have reflected on the unrepentant criminal who hung alongside Jesus, and now we will turn our thoughts towards the second criminal, the one who recognised something of who Jesus was.

This exchange is only mentioned in Luke's Gospel, where we read, "Two other men, both criminals, were also led out with him to be executed. When they came to the place called the Skull, they crucified him there, along with the criminals—one on his right, the other on his left. Jesus said, 'Father, forgive them, for they do not know what they are doing.' And they divided up his clothes by casting lots. The people stood watching, and the rulers even sneered at him. They said, 'He saved others; let him save himself if he is God's Messiah, the Chosen One.' The soldiers also came up and mocked him. They offered him wine vinegar and said, 'If you are the king of the Jews, save yourself.' There was a written notice above him, which read: this is the king of the Jews. One of the criminals who hung there hurled insults at him: 'Aren't you the Messiah? Save yourself and us!' But the other criminal rebuked him. 'Don't you fear God,' he said, 'since you are under the same sentence? We are punished justly, for we are getting what our deeds deserve. But this man has done nothing wrong.' Then he said, 'Jesus, remember me when you come into your kingdom.' Jesus answered him, 'Truly I tell you, today you will be with me in paradise'" (Luke 23:32 – 43).

This story is far easier than the last reflection; it is filled with hope and promise even amidst intense pain. While the other criminal thought only of himself, this one thinks of Jesus. Even in this terrible situation, with every fibre of his being in pain, he speaks in defence of Jesus: "We are getting what we deserve, but this man has done nothing wrong." It was an admission that Jesus was indeed who He said He was.

Interestingly, he wasn't seeking an escape; he didn't ask Jesus to save him or to end his suffering. He admitted that he deserved his punishment and, at the same time, proclaimed that he is a God-fearer, affirming that God is who He claims to be. He recognised that Jesus will ascend into His Kingdom.

And then these beautiful, reassuring words of Jesus: "Truly I tell you, today you will be with me in paradise" (Luke 23:32 – 43). Did any words in any situation ever offer such peace and reassurance?

This might be one of those moments when we find ourselves doing mental somersaults. What did it mean by "today", considering that we know Jesus died, was buried and would rise again on the third day? I believe we must recognise that Jesus existed both within and beyond time. Indeed, for this man, this would be the day on which he would rise again in God's heavenly kingdom. What can we learn from this man? That it's never too late and that we can leave things to the very last moment? That would be a dangerous game to play, considering that none of us knows the hour of our passing.

No, there is something about this man that suggests he may have known more about Jesus than merely their encounter on their crosses. Firstly, this man was a God-fearer; secondly, he understood aspects of the Kingdom that Jesus often spoke of and he recognised Jesus as innocent.

We know that, with his dying breath, he sought to protect Jesus and also tried to persuade the other criminal to change his heart. At a moment when even speaking was painful and laboured, these acts demonstrated selflessness and generosity. Jesus values a generous heart, one that considers others above oneself. Aside from expressing his heart, this man did absolutely nothing to enter the kingdom of God. I sometimes think I forget that I can do nothing to earn the love of God; He looks at my heart, not my actions. Although often my actions may reflect my heart, it is not the "doing" that He values.

The global pandemic highlighted the stark contrast between those for whom self-preservation was paramount in their thoughts and actions and those who rose to the challenge with love, compassion and extraordinary generosity towards others.

As a carer shielding a vulnerable family member and remaining in complete lockdown, I felt deeply frustrated at my inability to contribute more actively. Accepting generous help from others in various forms was humbling, but it made me realise that even in a state of helplessness (like being nailed to a cross), one's heart attitude is everything.

As we contemplate this self-confessed criminal whose act of selfless love touched the heart of Jesus, perhaps you too feel constrained in what you can "do". While you take time to reflect now, once again, there are different options available.

Quiet Reflection

Reread the passage Luke 23:32 – 43 and, once again, endeavour to imagine yourself in the position of the criminal. What thoughts come to mind as you do this?

You might wish to remember the first time you acknowledged that Jesus was Lord. How could you reaffirm that acknowledgement now? Take a moment to thank Jesus that there is nothing you can do to make Him love you more than He already does.

You might consider expressing gratitude for those who are a blessing in your life or for those you see giving selflessly to others. Pray that today they may receive an even greater blessing in return.

Session 4: Jesus

It is fitting that we conclude our Holy Week reflections with the final One who bore the cross. We consider Jesus, the One who, in obedience to His Father, chose the path of the cross for us, bearing the penalty we deserve, who took our guilt and shame and paid the ultimate price for us.

In a sense, there is nothing new under the sun; everything that could have been said has been said. If you have been reading the Gospel accounts of Jesus's passion over these last few days, you are likely in awe of what Jesus endured, both intentionally and steadfastly.

As we have considered Simon of Cyrene and the two criminals crucified alongside Jesus, along with the circumstances surrounding them, I would like us to reflect for a few moments on the significance of what brought Jesus to this place. Prophetic fulfilment, of course—God's plan to rescue humankind. But what were some of the actual human elements that contributed to this? It's easy for us to be bystanders and blame the Pharisees, the high priest or Pilate, but what motivated their actions and decisions?

Early on in the Gospels, we read that "the crowds were amazed at his teaching, because he taught as one who had authority, and not as their leaders of the law" (Matthew 7:28 – 29). We know for a fact that for those who had made a profession of teaching, this young nobody from Nazareth instilled quite a sense of jealousy. Can you imagine their indignation as He, too, gathered a group of disciples around Him who seemed to hang on His every word? I wonder if you have ever felt a twinge of envy towards someone who has performed better than you or achieved what you had not. I know I certainly have.

Some valued the traditions and intricate details of the law rather than understanding the essence of the law and the One who had given it. You will remember Jesus's disciples picking the ears of corn on the Sabbath for a quick snack, which was considered work, or Jesus showing compassion and healing on the Sabbath, causing a great stir and considerable anger. Do you ever prioritise playing it safe over stepping out in compassion? I know I have.

As we examine Jesus's jumped-up trial, we observe Caiaphas and the chief priests seeking false evidence as they felt profoundly threatened and fearful of losing their authority and status. Too many people were following this Jesus, and their actions thus reflect a desire to protect themselves. Then there is Pilate, who even ignored his wife's pleas because he was so concerned about staying on the right side of the powerful influence of the Jewish authorities. He washed his hands, saying, "Not my problem, not my responsibility." Have you ever allowed your desire for popularity to override your judgement regarding doing the right thing?

And what about the soldiers who flogged Him and mocked Him? Who jeered and laughed at Him? Here were men who were constantly under orders, at the beck and call of others, suddenly having someone they could push around. Were they jumping on a bandwagon, delighted to finally be above someone else in the pecking order and unleashing all kinds of frustrations? Perhaps they simply savoured the sheer cruelty of the moment.

And what about the apparent fickleness of the crowd? Less than a week before, they had been hailing Him as their Messiah while waving palm branches and welcoming Him into the streets of Jerusalem, and yet now they shouted, "Crucify!" Perhaps these were not the same individuals. There would have been thousands milling about the streets during these holy days, and perhaps a carefully chosen and manipulated crowd was present.

It is easy to imagine that everyone around Jesus was thoroughly unworthy and had malicious intentions, but we know that is not the case. We have witnessed the criminal alongside Jesus who spoke selflessly in His defence. We might also consider Mary worshipping Jesus as she anointed His feet with perfume just a few days earlier. There would have been many God-fearing Jews in Jerusalem at that time, and yet somehow many of them missed their Messiah, the very One they had been waiting for.

Life remains much the same today, doesn't it? The good and the bad continue to muddle along together. There are those who know and love Jesus, those who don't and those who may never have heard of Him. For many years, I believed I was a Christian purely because I lived in England. I grew up in an era when Religious Education (RE) lessons predominantly covered Bible stories, and our daily school assemblies included a hymn, a prayer and a brief reflection. However, I had no understanding that I could know this Jesus for myself and cultivate a personal relationship with Him. It was only when I encountered Christians who truly knew Him and whose hearts had been transformed by Him that I recognised what I was missing and what I had failed to perceive.

As I began to understand that Jesus had died for me, opening a path for my forgiveness and transformation and allowing me to have a constant and personal relationship with Him, my eyes were opened and life truly began. I grew to love reading my Bible and realised that every word was vibrant and true. You, too, may enjoy a life-transforming relationship with the One who died for you.

As we take time this Holy Week, let us once again stand at the foot of the cross and "fix our eyes on Jesus, the pioneer and perfector of faith. For the joy set before him he endured the cross, scorning its shame, and sat down at the right hand of the throne of God. Consider Him who endured such opposition from sinners so that you will not grow weary and lose heart (Hebrews 12:2 – 3).

Quiet Reflection

Reread the account of the crucifixion from whichever Gospel you choose. As much as possible, allow the enormity of what Jesus endured to resonate with you.

Take time for confession to Jesus, especially if any of the various scenarios resonate with you.

How do the burdens you may be carrying in some small way reflect the burdens that Jesus bore on that day? Speak to Him about the things that weigh you down.

Lamenting (weeping with those who weep) is not something that comes easily to many of us. Picture yourself in the position of John or Mary, and let your tears flow if necessary.

Give thanks to Jesus for His wonderful love for you and all humanity!

Resource 6

Jesus Appears to the Disciples

Session 1: Jesus Appears amid Trauma

Read John 20:19 – 23.

Given the enormity of this encounter, surprisingly few details are provided in this account. It reads more like a telegram.

The doors were locked; yet He appeared.

They were afraid; yet Jesus said, "Peace."

They were only overjoyed after they had seen His wounds. What happened before? More terror? Checking the locks?

He breathed on them—you need to be close to someone to feel their breath. Today is an opportunity to draw that close to Jesus as well.

I would like us to begin by considering the state the disciples were in.

They were locked inside out of fear of the Jewish leaders, even though it was the Roman authorities who had carried out the actual crucifixion.

Until the time of Jesus's arrest, they walked freely and openly associated with Him. However, at the moment of His arrest, except for Peter and John, they all fled. It would not be an exaggeration to say that they had been traumatised by the events of the past few days. They had given up their jobs and livelihoods; history does not reveal the impact that their following Jesus had on their families. We know for a fact that they were not all single young men, yet they and therefore their families had sacrificed everything to follow the One who had been betrayed, beaten and crucified.

What thoughts were they grappling with? Had they believed a falsehood? Had they been completely misled? Did they also ponder the question, "He saved others, but he couldn't save Himself?" Were they angry? Embarrassed by their foolishness? Feeling betrayed themselves perhaps?

What was happening in that locked room? Were they arguing among themselves? (They'd done plenty of that when Jesus was alive, too.) Some were likely silent and brooding over the events. Some may have felt ashamed for having run away. Others probably wanted to hear John repeat how Jesus had spoken from the cross and how He'd died. I'd like to think that John was a reassuring voice amid their pain, but perhaps some thought John and Peter had lost the plot, claiming they'd found the tomb empty. Had they even begun to consider what to do next?

Whatever was occurring, they were all afraid. They had openly associated with Jesus, and the Jews who had condemned Him also had the power to destroy them too.

It is into that context that Jesus comes and says, "Peace."

He speaks peace to their fears.

He speaks peace to their confusion.

He speaks peace to their pain and disappointment.

He speaks peace to their anger (towards individuals as well as the injustice).

I wonder what tone of voice He used. Was it a powerful, loud voice, as He had spoken to the storm when they were terrified by His authority over the weather? Was it loud and deliberate? Or was it filled with love and compassion? Was it soft and gentle?

Can you imagine the response? Were they silenced by Him, halted in their various mental tracks? Were they terrified once more? Did they feel hot and cold at the same time? A goose-bump moment. Yes, probably all of the above.

As Jesus steps into the disciples' chaos, He shows them His hands and side, proof that it truly is Him. It is only at that moment that their terror turns to joy. The relief! The delight! The whooping and cheering! Did they hug Him or fall back in wonder? What is your response to meeting Jesus? One thing is certain: it cannot be indifference.

As we take time to be still now, allow Jesus to enter that space with you. Do you have a place of trauma or chaos? Deep questions that you are uncertain how to express? Do you possess, so to speak, a locked room within you, a space that you keep concealed?

Quiet Reflection

Reread John 20:19 – 20 several times, allowing the scene to gradually take shape in your mind. What do you observe? Where are you positioned in the room? What is your reaction to seeing Jesus appear?

Do you have a place of trauma or chaos? Deep questions that you may not even know how to articulate? Do you possess, as it were, a locked room within you—a place that you keep hidden because opening it would be too terrifying? If you feel able, acknowledge those feelings and try to imagine Jesus stepping in and speaking "Peace" to you.

Session 2: Jesus Shares the Holy Spirit

Read John 20:21 – 22.

The disciples have experienced a rollercoaster of emotions, shifting from fear and terror to sheer jubilation and from desolation to wonder.

And again, Jesus says, "Peace." It's almost as if He's saying, "Calm yourselves, guys; this was prophesied. I too told you many times that this would happen; what's the big deal?"

I have more to tell you. It's important; please pay attention and be calm!

"As the Father has sent me, I am sending you" (John 20:21). Does it mean that, for the purpose for which the Father sent me, I am sending you? Well, through the power of His Spirit, we can do the same things—we can bring peace and reassurance to people, share the message of Good News with those who don't know and even pray for the healing of the sick and the raising of the dead. However, we certainly cannot and do not need to be the sacrifice and break the power of death. Perhaps it concerns the "how" He sent Him rather than the "what" that He sent him to do.

Perhaps we could interpret it differently. "As the Father", meaning "in the same way that the Father sent me, I am sending you." In that same manner. What does that mean?

John 3:16 famously tells us that "God so loved the world that He gave his one and only Son." The Father sent Jesus out of love. It is from this profound love for the world that Jesus was sent. It is that same overwhelming love for the world with which Jesus was sent to them and is now sending us as well. Love is the driving force.

Interpreting it this way illuminates our understanding in a completely different manner: God's love for them and His love for the world.

The second aspect of these two verses that I want us to consider is this: "He breathed on them" (John 20:22). What did that look like? Once more, we are somewhat short on detail. Was it a puff in the face? Was it akin to mouth-to-mouth resuscitation? Probably not. Does it simply mean He was so close to them that they could feel His breath? Do you remember the woman with the continuous bleeding who believed that if she merely touched Jesus she would be healed? The sheer power of Jesus's presence was overwhelming. Did He embrace them? We have no idea, but we know it was both an intimate moment and a deliberate act—an imparting of the Holy Spirit. Presumably, it was not the grand, dramatic event that it was at Pentecost when fire descended upon their heads and they began to speak in different languages. Nonetheless, He blessed them with the Holy Spirit right then and there.

We may focus on the Spirit's arrival at Pentecost and nearly overlook this moment; however, it was also a deeply profound occasion. It can be alarming how swiftly we read verses and miss the enormity of what was unfolding.

Effectively, Jesus was saying to them all, "I am sending you into the world, amongst people that I love, and I am equipping you and empowering you with my love and with my presence, to go and be my ambassador, my representative. The Father sent me with and in love, and He filled me with the Holy Spirit; now I am sending you in love and equipped in exactly the same way, filled with the Holy Spirit."

I'm unsure what to say other than WOW!

Quiet Reflection

Reread John 20:21 – 22 several times. Again, try to visualise the scene, being mindful of all your senses.

Allow the significance of what Jesus was saying and doing to fill you afresh today.

What does this mean to you? You may wish to journal your response to Him.

Allow yourself to be filled with awe and wonder.

Session 3: The Tricky Subject of Forgiveness

Read John 20:23.

Of all the things Jesus might have said or discussed at this point—perhaps about loving Him, remaining close to Him or the necessity of heeding the Holy Spirit's counsel—some key points on living filled with the Spirit could have been helpful, don't you think?

Instead, the only recorded element within this telegram is related to forgiveness. Why is that, unless the room was perhaps filled with unforgiveness?

In addition to their evident distress and trauma concerning Jesus's betrayal and crucifixion, the agony of his fabricated charges and brutal death, there was another significant issue affecting them all: another loss, another betrayal, another stream of questions.

Until Jesus's arrest, they had all walked freely and openly, participating in his itinerant ministry. It had been a very public association, but now they were cowering behind closed doors, and it was one of their own who had brought about this change. It was Judas who had betrayed them all, not just Jesus.

Judas was entrusted with the money bags and was presumably well-regarded by all the disciples. He had been with them for the three years they spent together. They must have shared laughter and jokes as well as the more serious matters that a group of men encounters while living life together. Judas was one of them, or at least he had been.

Can you imagine what the conversations were like regarding Judas? The anger, disbelief and self-questioning—"What did we miss? What did we fail to notice?" The desire for an explanation—"How could this have happened? How could he have done this?" Perhaps even thoughts, spoken or unspoken, of revenge?

It was in this highly-charged atmosphere that Jesus spoke these words: "If you forgive anyone's sins, their sins are forgiven; if you do not forgive them, they are not forgiven" (John 20:23).

Wow, what power! Yet the reality is that only Jesus has the authority to forgive us our sins, and only He has the right to judge. But that is not the full story.

If you consider it, and if we are honest with ourselves, we frequently judge others. We may spend a great deal of time and energy rehearsing the wrongs done to ourselves or others. What Jesus is saying here then perhaps is, "Let go of the wrongs of others. Forgive those who have got it wrong." If you reflect on the parable of the unmerciful servant (Matthew 18:21 – 25), Jesus illustrates that when we harbour unforgiveness and pass judgement on others, it is ultimately us who suffer. Moreover, we may not have truly experienced His forgiveness ourselves.

Jesus recognised that these men could not advance in their lives or their ministry while still harbouring anger and unforgiveness, not only towards Judas but also towards the Jewish and Roman authorities, the soldiers who had mocked and tortured him and so on. Unforgiveness cripples us regardless of whether it also impairs the wrongdoers.

Jesus says this after He has empowered them with the Holy Spirit. By ourselves, we may struggle to find it in our hearts to forgive, but the Holy Spirit will empower and equip us to let go of our desire for revenge or to get even.

Furthermore, without it, as the parable clearly demonstrates, we also cut ourselves off from a relationship with the Father.

It's a challenging matter, but it is vital to our well-being. There is a much-misused phrase, "forgive and forget", but nowhere does Jesus instruct us to forget. What forgiveness does for each of us is alleviate the pain associated with the memory. For many, forgiveness is a journey, not an instant, one-off solution. If the person involved is still alive, they may continue to cause you pain; furthermore, as new memories surface, you might need to keep practising forgiveness with the Holy Spirit's guidance and encouragement. There is so much more to discuss regarding this. An excellent booklet on this subject is 'The Power of Forgiveness' by John and Carol Arnott.

Perhaps you feel this is not relevant to you and that you are at peace with everyone. Wonderful! However, please be open to asking Jesus to reveal whether you are harbouring anything against anyone.

If you are struggling, a good first step is to ask God to help you be willing to undergo a change of heart and to experience His wonderful forgiveness anew.

Quiet Reflection

Reread John 20:23 and meditate on the words.

Express your deep gratitude to Jesus for your personal forgiveness. How might this change your attitude towards others?

You may already be aware of someone you need to forgive and release from your judgement. If not, sit quietly and ask Jesus to show you if there is anyone or any injustice that troubles you. In your mind, take them to the foot of the cross and "hand them over" to Jesus.

Resource 7
Zacchaeus

Read Luke 19:1 – 10.

Session 1: Seeing Jesus

Read Luke 19:1 – 4.

Zacchaeus had a problem; he wanted to see Jesus, but he couldn't. There were several reasons for this. Primarily, he was too short to see over the crowds surrounding him. Perhaps more subtly, the people in the crowd would not only have made no room for him, but they would most likely have actively and aggressively blocked his way.

What about us? Many people I speak to have a problem: they want to see Jesus, but they cannot. Obstacles get in the way:

- "My schedule is too busy."

- "My bed is too warm; if I stay, I risk falling back to sleep."

- "Sometimes, other people get in the way."

- "I'm afraid of exposure."

- Maybe even there is a fear that He won't speak.

Zacchaeus did two rather surprising things: he ran and climbed a tree. In that culture, it was considered very undignified for an adult to run, and tree climbing was generally viewed as an activity for children.

Both of these issues highlight the desperation that motivated Zacchaeus. He was propelled by a deep and intense desire to see Jesus.

There may be occasions when we, too, must take drastic action, as Zacchaeus did, in order to see Jesus. Perhaps your presence here today represents that drastic action.

As we enter this period of quiet, let us reflect on our eagerness or desperation to see Jesus, or potentially, our lack of it.

Quiet Reflection

Reread Luke 19:4 a number of times. Does any word or phrase stand out to you?

Imagine yourself in the tree alongside Zacchaeus. What exactly was he observing, and what did he see when he looked at Jesus? What was Jesus doing before He called him down? What were the crowds around Him doing and saying? Can you envision the expressions on their faces?

What or who prevents you from seeing Jesus clearly?

Zacchaeus did two very counter-cultural things to see Jesus. What do you need to do to see Jesus?

How extreme are you prepared to be? Do you need to forgive anyone who may have got in your way? Could you be obstructing or hindering someone else from encountering Jesus? Allow the Holy Spirit to reveal your attitudes, judgements or preconceived notions about others. Repent and confess these to Him.

Session 2: Being Seen by Jesus

Read Luke 19:1 – 7.

I wonder how long Zacchaeus had been in the tree before Jesus reached him. A few minutes? Was he still out of breath? Or had he been observing Jesus from a distance as He stopped and spoke with people, healing them and giving them His full attention? Perhaps he had been up there for quite some time before Jesus came level with him.

There is something intrinsically beautiful about this moment of encounter. Throughout his working life, Zacchaeus had been both hated and despised by his fellow Jews. He was viewed not only as a traitor, collaborating with the Roman regime, but also as someone suspected of being a cheat and a thief, helping himself to additional funds from the taxes he collected across the region. As a chief tax collector, he would have had others working under him, and whether this was actually true or merely a generalisation that "all tax collectors must be on the fiddle" remains unknown. However, based on his later confession, it may indeed have been the case. The general population wanted nothing to do with him, yet there was Jesus speaking to him by name, his actual name, not the labels everyone else placed upon him. Ironically, the meaning of Zacchaeus in Hebrew is purity or innocence, which feels a million miles away from anything anyone else might have called him.

The crowd perceived only a filthy, deceitful cheat. There was likely much jeering and laughter as they saw him climbing the tree, with people pointing and mocking him. Yet, amidst it all, Jesus looked up and spoke to him by name. Not only that, He called him down so that he could host Jesus in his own home. How extraordinary is that? Can you imagine how Zacchaeus felt in that moment?

So what did Jesus see that the crowds did not? Jesus saw someone who was desperately seeking a relationship with Him. He observed an individual who was willing to be undignified to draw closer to Him. Jesus cherishes a hungry and thirsty heart.

In John 7:37 – 38, we read that Jesus said, "Let anyone who is thirsty come to me and drink. Whoever believes in me, as scripture has said, streams of living water will flow from within them." Jesus wished to satisfy the hunger he perceived in Zacchaeus. Zacchaeus came down and "welcomed Him gladly" (Luke 19:6). Just reading that fills my heart with joy. Jesus can change and transform us simply by speaking our names and drawing us into His presence. What a wonderful interaction!

As we enter this second period of quiet, let us take a moment to reflect on the beauty of this moment; it is as if you can almost feel the weight lifting from Zacchaeus's shoulders. More importantly, let us contemplate the wonder of who Jesus is and His ability to perceive when we feel hidden or overlooked by others.

Quiet Reflection

Reread Luke 19: 1 – 6 and pay special attention to any words or phrases that stand out to you. Spend some time reflecting on them. What might Jesus wish to convey to you?

When Jesus looked up at Zacchaeus, He perceived something entirely different from what the people saw. Ask Jesus what He sees when He looks at you. Perhaps imagine Him speaking your name.

Jesus asked to share a meal with Zacchaeus, perhaps even to stay overnight. He was an honoured guest at Zacchaeus's table. Where do you engage with Jesus? Where might Jesus desire to sit and connect with you?

Session 3: Being Changed by Jesus

Read Luke 19:1 – 10.

The mood of the crowd swiftly shifts from likely jeering and laughter to horror and indignation as they realise that Jesus chose "this sinner" out of all of them to go to his home for tea. I wonder what their inner reactions were because, let's face it, they had all come out to see Jesus for themselves—some because they sought healing, some out of mere curiosity and perhaps others because their esteemed teachers of the law vehemently disagreed with Him, prompting them to hear Him for themselves. Of them all, Jesus chose the one who was despised by the rest.

For Jesus's critics, this choice of dinner guest merely confirmed their prejudice; here was a man who consorted with the wrong people, a most irreligious act that showed further disrespect to their own teachers of the law. For those in the crowd feeling crushed by the tyranny of Rome, Jesus was showing favour to someone who merely added to their oppression. For most of those present, it was a truly confusing moment; no wonder there was muttering.

It is hard to know whether, at that moment of encounter, Zacchaeus expresses this apparent and sudden change of attitude. Did it occur then or as a result of their conversation over dinner, since Jesus's response seems to take place in his house? In our minds, the second option may appear more logical; it is only as we interact with Jesus that our hearts are convicted and changed. However, the way it is written suggests it was an instant reaction. But—and it is a significant but—there is an interesting twist in this account. In some translations, perhaps most notably the King James Version, the tense of this sentence is present and ongoing. "And Zacchaeus stood, and said unto the Lord: Behold, Lord, the half of my goods I give to the poor; and if I have taken any thing from any man by false accusation, I restore him fourfold" (Luke 19:8 KJV). This would change the narrative completely.

Far from being the sinner that everyone had labelled him, perhaps this man was truly righteous and living up to his name of purity and innocence. In making such a declaration, was he defending himself against the accusations of the crowd? What a change in perspective on a story we thought we knew! Was the story actually told to highlight the prejudice and judgemental attitudes of the crowd who saw only a dirty, rotten sinner?

When Jesus sends out the 72 on their mission endeavours (Luke 10: 5 – 7), He instructs them to find people of peace with whom to eat and stay. Did Jesus know that Zacchaeus was himself a "person of peace", indeed a righteous man, and therefore what better place to stay and relax after a long day of ministry? This is purely conjecture.

Whichever way we consider this, Jesus affirms two things (Luke 10:9). Firstly, that salvation has come to the house because He Himself has been welcomed there, and secondly, that Zacchaeus too is a true son of Abraham. As someone who had been constantly rejected by his fellow Jews due to his choice of occupation, Jesus says of him, "Here is one who truly walks in the footsteps of Abraham because of his faith and righteousness." Luke 19:10 tells us that Jesus came to "seek and to save the lost." If

Zacchaeus was a thief and a cheat, then truly he was transformed that day; but if he was a righteous man who had been rejected by his own people, that isolation must surely have created an incredible sense of aloneness and lost-ness. In calling him down from the tree, Jesus found him and restored him to his people.

I did not intend to create confusion, and I hope you feel able to explore this story as you wish. Either way, there are valuable lessons for us to learn and powerful insights that the Lord can share with us. As we enter this final period of quiet, let us set aside any sense of confusion and allow the Lord to reveal to us what He will.

Quiet Reflection

Sit with the passage and let yourself be immersed in the drama of the story. Who are you, where are you and what do you feel as you listen to this dialogue?

Conversations with Jesus can be profoundly personal and private. We do not know how the dinner conversation unfolded between Jesus and Zacchaeus, nor is it ours to know. Take time to engage in a personal conversation with Him now. You may wish to ask Jesus if there is any way in which you could be blinded to someone whom He may wish to encounter. Meeting Jesus transformed Zacchaeus and led to an immediate confession. Is there anything you might find beneficial to confess to Jesus?

Do you ever feel isolated or lost? As you seek Jesus, can you hear Him speak your name?

Resource 8

God's Workmanship

Focal Point

As a potential focal point, you might consider incorporating some craft tools, such as chisels surrounded by wood shavings or paints and paintbrushes alongside a simple sketch.

Introduction

"For we are God's handiwork, created in Christ Jesus to do good works, which God prepared in advance for us to do" (Ephesians 2:10).

This is one verse but in three parts, making it ideal for a Quiet Day. In the first session, we are going to explore what it means to be God's workmanship. In the second session, we will discover what it means to be created in Christ and what good works might involve. Lastly, we will examine what God may have prepared for us.

Ephesians 2:10 is often quoted in isolation, but for any verse that begins with "For" or "Therefore", we do well to ask the question, "What is it there for?" i.e. What is the context of this verse? As it does not stand alone, it is very much part of whatever precedes it. Let's read those preceding verses. "As for you, you were dead in your transgressions and sins, in which you used to live when you followed the ways of this world and of the ruler of the kingdom of the air, the spirit who is now at work in those who are disobedient. All of us also lived among them at one time, gratifying the cravings of our flesh and following its desires and thoughts. Like the rest, we were by nature deserving of wrath. But because of his great love for us, God, who is rich in mercy, made us alive with Christ even when we were dead in transgressions—it is by grace you have been saved. And God raised us up with Christ and seated us with him in the heavenly realms in Christ Jesus, in order that in the coming ages he might show the incomparable riches of his grace, expressed in his kindness to us in Christ Jesus. For it is by grace you have been saved, through faith—and this is not from yourselves, it is the gift of God—not by works, so that no one can boast. For we are God's handiwork, created in Christ Jesus to do good works, which God prepared in advance for us to do" (Ephesians 2:1 – 10).

This provides a helpful perspective on this verse rather than allowing it to stand on its own.

Session 1: For We Are God's Workmanship

Have you ever created something, perhaps a piece of woodwork, a painting or even a photograph that you have been so pleased with that, despite some minor imperfections, you have proudly displayed it somewhere? I remember someone once saying, "If

God had a fridge, your picture would be on it." We are told in Genesis 1:31 that "God saw all that He had made and it was good," but of man, whom He had made in His own image, it was very good.

Are we ever at risk of saying, "Yes—all except me!"? How many of us look in the mirror each morning and exclaim, "Wow, now that is something truly amazing!"?

We have straight hair and long for curly hair, while those with curly hair yearn for straight locks. We look at our faces and feel that there's too much hair. We are simply never quite satisfied.

And that merely scratches the surface of our physical bodies. What about our unique, individual gifts—the abilities we possess, our creative talents with words, music, numbers, computing or interpersonal skills? Often the things we are gifted at seem to come naturally to us, and we may take them for granted; yet, when we observe the gifts of others, we may feel less capable. What of our emotional well-being and mental capacity, alongside everything else that swirls within our minds and hearts? We are indeed fearfully and wonderfully made, but somewhere along the way, we may have lost the wonder of our uniqueness. Perhaps we have diminished our confidence in our abilities, or maybe we look at others and feel as though we have been short-changed or lack some vital ingredient.

Why might we have issues?

Firstly, we may have been criticised or we may have never received the encouragement we needed to excel. Negative words can have an incredibly profound and crippling effect on us. I remember an elderly lady attending a painting session I was running. Her first words were, "Don't expect anything of me. I can't paint." After a couple of hours, she produced perhaps the best artwork of us all. She confessed that as a child, her mother had criticised a painting she had proudly brought home and thrown it in the bin. She had never painted again until that day. What joy and talent had been robbed from her?

Other significant barriers to feeling comfortable in our own skin and accepting who we are may include comparison and fear.

Comparison, Have you ever said or perhaps just thought to yourself, "I am not as gifted as him", "I couldn't do what she does", "I'm not as fun to be around", "I'm not as attractive, not as sporty," "I don't earn as much," "I'm not as pastoral or wise..."? Fill in your own blanks. Such thoughts can lead us to conclude that we are somehow less than others. We focus on what we can't do rather than rejoicing in our own particular gifts and abilities.

Another barrier is fear: "What will people think of me?" "Will people question my motives?" "What if I fail?" "If people knew my background..." "If they knew what I am really like..." Fear of others' judgement, expectation or even our own expectations can prevent us from attempting something or cause us to stop doing something at the first sign of difficulty. Whatever the root cause may be, the result is that we do not flourish and live in the fullness that God intended for us as part of His precious creation.

The enemy continuously seeks ways to undermine God's creation, and he can be quite subtle in his methods. There is no "one size fits all" approach to his scheming.

I remember two ladies in a group at a ministry school; both had issues regarding self-worth, yet each expressed them in completely opposite ways. One wore excessive make-up in an attempt to hide who she believed she was while the other wore no make-up at all, feeling unworthy of making herself look good. By the end of the ministry school, both ladies received such healing that one was able to go out make-up free, and the other began to take pride in her appearance. Both were able to rejoice in the individuals God had created them to be.

One way to overcome these unhelpful thoughts about ourselves is to adopt a grateful attitude. We have so much to appreciate; regardless of our circumstances, we can always find something to be thankful for. When someone close to me sustained life-changing injuries, I remember being grateful for the ability to perform the simplest tasks, such as walking across the room or carrying a mug of tea—so many things I had taken for granted until that point in my life.

Let's turn to Psalms 139:1 – 16. None of us is an accident or a mistake, even if we, or our parents, believe otherwise. God Himself knew us and planned us; we are His workmanship, known and created by Him.

We are the apple of His eye (Zechariah 2:8).

He rejoices over us with singing (Zephaniah 3:17).

We are God's workmanship, and anything we do to diminish ourselves actually diminishes God's creative ability. As we read at the beginning, we were dead in our sins, but not any more. We have been affected and broken by the world, yet we are being transformed by the renewing of our minds (Romans 12:2). Therefore, as we enter this first period of quiet, let us allow God, by His Spirit, to work in us, renewing and transforming us in any areas where we have thought less of ourselves than God does. This should be done not in a proud manner but with humility and wonder.

Quiet Reflection

Take time to marvel in the wonder of God's workmanship.

Take some time to be still with God and thank Him for creating you—your body, your unique gifts and abilities, your character and so on. You may wish to list them as you express your gratitude.

Use Psalms 139:23 – 24 as a prayer, asking God to reveal any false beliefs you hold about yourself that diminish His glory within you or any fears that prevent you from being fully you. Confess these challenges and ask God to impart truth into that area of your life.

Session 2: Created in Christ Jesus

Read Ephesians 2:10.

If we are already aware that we are God's workmanship, what does it mean to be created in Christ Jesus? It seems like a contradiction or a double statement. The Message version of this whole passage is very helpful:

"Now God has us where he wants us, with all the time in this world and the next to shower grace and kindness upon us in Christ Jesus. Saving is all his idea, and all his work. All we do is trust him enough to let him do it. It's God's gift from start to finish! We don't play the major role. If we did, we'd probably go around bragging that we'd done the whole thing! No, we neither make nor save ourselves. God does both the making and saving. He creates each of us by Christ Jesus to join him in the work he does, the good work he has gotten ready for us to do, work we had better be doing." (Ephesians 2: 7-10, MSG).

God created us, and Jesus saved us. He loves each of us so much that He could not bear for us to be lost in our sins, to die, to be separated from Him or to be out of relationship with Him—whatever phrase helps you grasp the depth of His love. So what is the implication of that? Is it simply that we will be seated with God in heavenly realms when we die, or is it possible that we can also be seated in heavenly realms now? Do you feel that you are living in heavenly realms now, or do you feel drained, overwhelmed and as if you are chasing your tail all at the same time?

I love this phrase: "For it is by grace you have been saved, through faith, and this not from yourselves, it is the gift of God—not by works so that no one can boast" (Ephesians 2:8 – 9). It is one of those verses that you can read and just breathe a big sigh of relief.

And yet, we then read that we are created to perform good works. Surely that presents a contradiction. We have just been told we cannot do anything to save ourselves.

The issue lies not in whether we carry out good works but rather in the motivation or inspiration with which we undertake them.

It has been my observation, both in my own life and in the lives of others, that having been saved by grace, through faith in Jesus and all the joy that brings, something changes. It may be so subtle that we don't notice it, but we can transition from that place of grace into a place of working for our salvation. A bit like the older brother in the parable of the prodigal son, who felt like he was a slave to the father. He had lost the joy of relationship with Him and became focused on the doing, not the being. And somewhere, the thought arises that God would be disappointed or wouldn't love us as much should we fail to meet every need that comes our way. The essence of this upcoming quiet time is to savour some "ahhh" moments and rest in the wonder of the verse, "For it is by grace you have been saved" (Ephesians 2:8).

Quiet Reflection

Meditate on Ephesians 2:8 – 9, rereading it repeatedly until it becomes part of your natural breathing rhythm. Rest in the wonder of what Jesus has done for you; rest in His love and complete acceptance.

If you find yourself feeling impatient to be "doing" something, you might like to reflect on your "good works" and consider your motivations. Is there anything that Jesus wants to say to you about these matters?

Session 3: God's Plans

Read Ephesians 2:10.

God made us; He prepared in advance for our salvation and has set good works before us. What does this reveal about God? He is a God of order, not of chaos. He is prepared. Events and opportunities do not enter our lives haphazardly or by chance.

He is aware of our weaknesses; however, he is even more familiar with our strengths, gifts and abilities, for He gave them to us. I genuinely believe that God wants us to enjoy life, to savour each moment and not to merely struggle through it. When we operate within our gifting—what we are good at or what "comes naturally" to us—we feel energised by our actions rather than depleted by them. I mentioned in an earlier chapter about my colleague at Ashburnham who did not feel able to give the notices while I found it difficult to be pastorally attentive to guests at a house party. Working outside our gifting can be challenging unless God grants us the strength to do so for a season.

He may also change us and shape us into the person He has always intended. When I first came to faith, I was incredibly shy. I used to hide in the kitchen to avoid conversations with others. At that time, I would never have imagined myself leading groups, preaching or even writing a book. Over time, as I stepped out in faith, God has enabled me to accomplish things beyond my wildest dreams. I have been saved to do the good works that God has prepared for me, and so have you. There is a commonly repeated phrase, although I do not know its origin: "God doesn't call the equipped; He equips the called." God often calls us or places a yearning in our hearts before equipping us for the journey.

Redeeming is a process. Through the guidance and prompting of the Holy Spirit, He works on us gradually, transforming our brokenness into His likeness. Thus, our good deeds flow from our resemblance to Jesus. His heart beats within ours, and as we find rest in Him, we will attune ourselves to His heart, remaining vigilant to the tasks He has set before us and to the wisdom needed to discern what is not our task. I find great comfort in the story early in Acts, right at the very beginning of the disciples' ministry. We are told of a man who had been crippled from birth, sitting every day on the way to the temple courts to beg from those going to pray. This suggests that Jesus would have walked by him.

Jesus did not heal everyone. God had planned and purposed for Peter and John to bring healing to him. For many in ministry, we recognise that we could work 24 hours a day and still not attend to everyone and every need around us. God never intended for us to do everything or to be run ragged, but He does have certain tasks for us to undertake, partnering with Him in His work.

He knows our strengths and weaknesses, yet He does not allocate tasks to us based on what we can manage. He has planned and purposed for us to undertake specific things, sometimes far beyond our capabilities (think of Moses, Gideon, David, Peter, Paul, William Wilberforce, Billy Graham, Jackie Pullinger, Heidi Baker, the list goes on). It is also interesting to note that Jesus did not choose Matthew, despite his accounting skills, to look after the money bag. He has had plans for you since before eternity to live, love and work in relationship with and in reliance on Him through His Holy Spirit. What an awesome God we serve!

There are potentially two different responses to consider during this time of quiet. You may be wondering what God has in store for you, or perhaps you are aware of it but are unsure of how to move forward. Alternatively, you may be feeling overwhelmed, as if you cannot take on anything else; perhaps God is urging you to let something go. However, please do not feel obligated to follow these suggestions.

Quiet Reflection

Sit quietly with Ephesians 2:10 for a while, asking God to reveal anything specific that He wishes for you to hear.

God is a God of order. Are you feeling overstretched by all that you are doing? Ask Him to guide you to a place of peace and order. Reflect on everything you do. Consider what energises you and which activities deplete your energy. Discuss your lists with God. Are you avoiding something that God has laid on your heart because it feels too daunting? Consider Gideon, hiding in fear, yet God called him "a mighty warrior". Or Peter, who even denied knowing Jesus, and yet it was upon him whom God said, "I will build my church."

Now, what is your issue? Speak to God about how He intends to assist you or at least show you the first step.

Resource 9

Harvest: Jesus is the Vine

Focal Point

A focal point for this reflection might be a picture or photograph of a vine, a tree or perhaps a bunch of grapes.

Read John 15:1 – 12.

Session 1: The Father is the Gardener

I wonder what first captures your attention as you read this passage. Is it the pain and discomfort of pruning or the joy of fruitfulness? Is it the wonder of knowing the Father is watching over you, the feeling Jesus being so close and connected or the fear of being placed on the rubbish heap for burning? Is it the joy of access in prayer through the Holy Spirit or the pain of prayer that has long gone unanswered? This passage may raise as many questions for us as it brings hope and joy. Today, you have the opportunity to ask those questions of Jesus and enjoy the wonder of the relationship we can cultivate with God the Trinity: Father, Son and Holy Spirit.

For this initial session, we will concentrate solely on the first verse. Let us begin by contemplating God the Father as the Gardener. I am an amateur gardener, with an emphasis on amateur. I LOVE gardening; it brings me immense joy. I adore spending time in my garden, observing everything and checking for buds and bugs. Rarely does a day go by without me wandering around the flower beds to see how everything is faring. I enjoy growing plants from seed or taking cuttings. I feel so excited when I see new shoots emerging or buds bursting open into beautiful blooms.

But it is true that I am also an optimistic gardener; I simply plant things and hope for the best, while a professional gardener would check the soil's acidity, ensure the position is just right—not too sunny or too shady—verify that the drainage suits the type of root system and so on.

I also don't like to prune my plants, although I know I have to at times. My philosophy is that if a plant or tree has put in considerable effort to grow, then who am I to cut it back? Meanwhile, a professional gardener will willingly prune excess growth to ensure vibrant flowers and fruit in the following seasons, as they understand that pruning enhances something that is already good, making it even better.

However, the truth is, whether amateur or professional, all gardeners love their gardens; they appreciate each individual plant, cherishing and nurturing it as best they can. I have never met a gardener who doesn't enjoy gardening.

How much more, then, will our Heavenly Father watch over each one of us, eager to see a new green shoot, thrilled when the flowers begin to open or when the fruit is set and ready to ripen? Furthermore, there is no place a gardener prefers to be than in a garden or, in this case, wandering through the vineyard to check on the vines.

A gardener has everything necessary at their disposal to ensure positive outcomes for each plant. They possess all the required equipment, understand the most beneficial environments, instinctively identify what may cause a plant to appear pale or wilt and take immediate remedial action simply because they want the plant to thrive.

Our Father is the Gardener of our souls. He constantly watches over us; He knows what we need. He takes delight in our growth, our blossoming and our fruitfulness, and He loves to be present with us through all the changing seasons of life. That is the heart of the Gardener: the flourishing of each plant is His joy, and the annual bringing in of the harvest is always anticipated with bated breath.

I love the image of entire families or communities gathered around a laden table after the grape harvest has been completed, often seated right in the heart of the vineyard. It's a lovely depiction of the joy of being present among the very vines that have produced the crop and will ultimately be transformed into wine.

As we enter a time of quiet now, let's take time to simply dwell on this image of the Father as the Gardener. Try not to think of yourself as the plant, wondering what needs to be trimmed or whether you require more compost; instead, focus on the wonder of God delighting in your company.

Quiet Reflection

You might consider rereading John 15:1 several times. Make a concerted effort not to contemplate the rest of the passage at this moment, but instead, focus solely on this one verse. What does that imagery look like in your mind?

Can you imagine the delight on the Gardener's face as He sees tiny buds or shoots of growth or as he checks to see how the fruit is ripening?

Take the time to thank God and to worship Him for the qualities or aspects of His character that this image evokes—nurture, care, desire for flourishing, delight, etc.

Session 2: Jesus is the Vine

The image of the vine was often used in the Old Testament to describe the people of Israel, but Jesus refers to Himself as the "true vine", in other words, the trustworthy and legitimate vine, the vine that would produce only good fruit.

A vine consists of the rootstock, the main stem or trunk and all the branches that bear the leaves and fruit. The entire plant possesses the same nature and characteristics.

Jesus, the true vine, has branches that are also the true vine—that's you and me. How extraordinary is that?

However, we must address the challenging topic of pruning. It is essential to understand that there is a distinction between cutting off unproductive branches (John 15:6) and the pruning of productive branches (John 15:2). These are entirely different processes.

The fruitless branches could possibly be likened to the goats in the parable of the sheep and the goats (Matthew 25:31 – 46), illustrating the distinction between those who are obedient to Jesus and those who are not. This serves as a stark warning about the impending judgement; however, Jesus reassures his disciples that they are part of the true vine, fruit-bearing branches (John 15:2), and reminds them to remain close to Him.

The metaphor of pruning is one we often use when discussing our spiritual journeys. I am sure it holds true for you, as it has for me, that there have been moments when something that seemed very fruitful was suddenly halted or ended in some way. In those moments, such occurrences can be quite painful; however, in the fullness of time, we discover that they have liberated us to pursue something even more fruitful or that we have learned a lesson that has led us to a greater degree of maturity. At times, pruning can seem harsh, but if we stay connected to the vine, if we walk closely with Jesus and submit to His guidance, we will find ourselves nourished and refreshed by Him. Over time, we will realise that we are growing more fruitfully once again.

What an extraordinary and powerful image this is—that we can be so connected with Jesus, like a branch on a vine. It is indistinguishable where one starts and the other stops, for they are all the same thing. Perhaps that feels too great a concept to comprehend, but the truth is that when the world looks at us, what they are seeing is a reflection of God. Jesus said in Matthew 5:16, "In the same way, let your light shine before others, that they may see your good deeds and glorify your Father in heaven." The more we spend time with Jesus, the more we reflect His character; likewise, the less we give Him our attention, the less we will be like Him.

Of course, productive branches can give rise to unnecessary side shoots, which also need to be removed and released.

As we enter this second period of quiet, let us focus on Jesus, the true vine, and reflect on the characteristics of Jesus's fruitfulness. What does it mean to be so attached to Him that we are one and the same?

Quiet Reflection

Reread John 15:1 – 5 slowly and prayerfully. What words resonate with you? Reflect on them and ask

God to reveal more. You may like to write in your journal what it means to you to be so attached to Jesus.

Instead of criticising yourself for your failings or shortcomings, have an honest and genuine conversation about any disconnection you may be experiencing. Make sure you listen rather than dominate the conversation.

Session 3: Fruitfulness

Read John 15:7 – 12.

It was challenging to determine where to stop reading. Verse 8 may appear to be the natural conclusion of the passage, but the following verses are simply wonderful and provide that additional bit of oomph we might need to motivate us towards fruitfulness; it felt wrong not to include them.

Let's begin with verse 7: "If you remain in me and my words remain in you, ask whatever you wish, and it will be done for you." This might seem like an open-ended invitation or perhaps something akin to the prosperity gospel. Alternatively, it could provoke numerous questions, especially if you have been asking repeatedly and...nothing!

When I was baptised, I was given a Bible verse that has remained one of my "life verses". Psalm 37:4 says, "Take delight in the Lord, and he will give you the desires of your heart." Over the years, I have come to realise the correlation between the first and second parts of this verse. It is as we "delight ourselves in the Lord", i.e. spend time in His company, listen to His voice and walk in obedience with Him, that the "desires of our hearts" increasingly change and align more closely with His heart. The things we want and long for are those that bring Him pleasure and delight.

Instead of merely fulfilling all our earthly desires, we aspire to see the hungry fed, justice served to the dispossessed and so forth. It is we who are transformed to be like Him, not the other way around. He is not some sort of celestial vending machine.

When we talk about being fruitful, I wonder what we really mean. Perhaps our minds jump to Galatians 5:22 – 23: "But the fruit of the Spirit is love, joy, peace, forbearance, kindness, goodness, faithfulness, gentleness and self-control." And indeed, these are all markers of a person who is seeking to live in step with the Holy Spirit's promptings. However, I remember being asked by a preacher, "What does an apple tree produce?" Of course, everyone answered, "Apples!" But the true answer is apple trees. While fruit may be delicious to eat, its true purpose is to reproduce—for the pips to fall into the ground and grow into healthy new trees.

Observing someone living in a way that their lives display "the various fruits of the spirit" is perhaps akin to gazing at a tree laden with beautiful fruit or even savouring its deliciousness. However, to be truly fruitful, we ought to witness a process of reproduction. Jesus told us in Matthew 28:19 − 20, "Therefore go and make disciples of all nations, baptising them in the name of the Father and of the Son and of the Holy Spirit, and teaching them to obey everything I have commanded you. And surely I am with you always, to the very end of the age." He expected us to witness reproduction, and we are here only because that reproductive process has continued through the centuries.

Please hear me when I say that this doesn't mean we must all rush out and become street-preaching evangelists; rather, it signifies that we should faithfully utilise all the gifts and talents that God has bestowed upon us to assist others in hearing and growing in their faith journey. Yes, some will be evangelists, but others will possess the gifts of teaching or pastoring, which are all essential for nurturing new disciples.

The true clue to being genuinely fruitful lies in reading these next verses: "As the Father has loved me, so have I loved you. Now remain in my love. If you keep my commands, you will remain in my love, just as I have kept my Father's commands and remain in his love. I have told you this so that my joy may be in you and that your joy may be complete. My command is this: Love each other as I have loved you" (John 15:9-12). As we recognise ourselves as being loved by our Heavenly Father and continue to love Jesus, while being guided by the Spirit, our lives will naturally draw people to God.

As we conclude with this final time of quiet, there are several options to consider.

Quiet Reflection

Consider how you "delight yourself in God". Ask Him if there are things you could do to make this a daily habit in some way. What does "remaining in His love" look like?

Reflect on how "the desires of your heart" have changed over time.

Ask God what it means to "love each other as He has loved you". Do specific individuals come to mind?

Who might you be helping to disciple?

Author Biography

Margaret has spent most of her adult life in Christian ministry and church leadership. Together with her husband, she helped lead the community at Ashburnham Place: Conference and Prayer Centre in East Sussex, where she had particular responsibility for the international young adult discipleship programme as well as helping to pioneer continuous gathered prayer amongst the staff team. More recently, she has been a Licensed Lay Minister in the Diocese of Rochester, where she was a member of the Spirituality Network, frequently leading Quiet Days and training others to do the same. Recently, she moved to Sheffield, where she continues her ministry of preaching, teaching and encouraging others.

About PublishU

PublishU enables you to tell your story or communicate your message by writing and publishing a book worldwide.

"I never thought I would be able to write a book, let alone in 100 days... now I'm asking what else have I told myself that I can't do that I actually can?'"

PublishU Author

To find out more visit

www.PublishU.com

Printed in Dunstable, United Kingdom